HEART AND

SEVEN SIGNS IN JOHN'S GOSPEL

MATTHEW: A STORY ABOUT JESUS

Andrew Facey

The Bible Reading Fellowship
OPENING THE BIBLE

Text copyright © Andrew Facey 1996

The author asserts the moral right to be
identified as the author of this work.

Published by
The Bible Reading Fellowship
Peter's Way, Sandy Lane West
Oxford OX4 5HG
ISBN 0 7459 2976 1
Albatross Books Pty Ltd
PO Box 320, Sutherland
NSW 2232, Australia
ISBN 0 7324 0949 7

First edition 1996
10 9 8 7 6 5 4 3 2 1 0

Acknowledgments
Unless otherwise stated, scripture is taken from
The New Revised Standard Version of the Bible
copyright © 1989 by the Division of Christian
Education of the National Council of the
Churches of Christ in the USA.

Scripture marked (NIV) taken from the Holy
Bible, New International Version, copyright ©
1973, 1978, 1984 by International Bible
Society. Used by permission of Hodder and
Stoughton Limited.

Extracts from *The Structure of Matthew's Gospel*
by David Bauer appear by permission of
Sheffield Academic Press

A catalogue record for this book is
available from the British Library

Printed and bound in Malta
by Interprint Limited

Contents

To my wife, Dr Jane Facey, whose sharp mind, penetrating comments,
unfailing support and loving encouragement continue to be a blessing to me.

ACKNOWLEDGMENTS

This material has all been 'road-tested' in a real, live church! My considerable thanks to the parish church of St John the Baptist, Egham, to Alistair Magowan, its Vicar, and to its Home Group Network, for allowing me the time to write this material and for being so gracious and encouraging in the use of it.

I am particularly indebted to D.R. Bauer's book, *The Structure of Matthew's Gospel* (Sheffield Academic Press, 1988) for offering the theological and textual framework on which the studies on Matthew's Gospel are based.

Introduction

Welcome to this book of home-group study material! Over the page, you will find some practical suggestions about how to use it. Immediately after that, you will find an introductory chapter on how to lead a study group.

The studies in John and those in Matthew are quite different from each other. It doesn't matter which you start with, but do think about it first. The paragraphs below will help you to decide.

Seven signs in John's Gospel

These studies are based around seven of John's 'signs' of Jesus' glory. The 'signs' point us towards a deeper appreciation of who Jesus is and what he came to do. Because the 'signs', as John relates them, are very visible, tangible, material things such as water, wine, bread and healing, the studies ask us to approach the text not only through our minds, but also engaging our senses and by using the material world around us. The aim is that by reading, studying, thinking, looking and tasting, group members will be drawn closer to Jesus, and that John's 'signs' will elicit a response from them, a response of dependence upon Jesus himself.

Matthew's Gospel: A story about Jesus

The studies in Matthew are quite different. The theme of the material is that Mattew's Gospel can profitably be read as a story, a story about Jesus' ministry. It is a ministry which involves contact with and opposition from the Jewish authorities. As we read about it, we discover Jesus to be the Son of God, sent with God's own authority, and yet sent to suffer and die on behalf of a stricken world.

Quite often study material on the Gospels is content to read a particular Gospel passage as a self-contained unit, and fails to relate the text in question to the rest of the Gospel. Not so these studies! The aim is to compare each of the seven passages we study to the rest of Matthew's Gospel and to ask what these passages are meant to achieve. By doing this we begin to put together a detailed picture of who Jesus is and what he came to do. And in the process we get to ask some quite incisive questions about what this may mean for the Church and for the world today.

How to use this study material

Each study session has:

• Study notes—leading group members through the session. This will be one or two double-pages, but very occasionally, three.

• Leader's notes—helping leaders prepare for each session and learn more about the Bible passage being studied.

Permission is given for the study notes in this book to be photo-copied for group use—so that each member may have a copy of the study notes to use and keep. The leader's notes and other contents of the book are excluded from this provision.

A space called 'Growth points' is provided in each study notes where group members may write in anything they want to take away with them from that session.

We recommend that everyone has a copy of the study notes at the beginning so they can follow it through together. But that is entirely up to you. You may prefer to give it out at the end, so that members can refresh their memories later.

The translation used is generally The New Revised Standard Version (NRSV) or New International Version (NIV). Use any translation that you and your group feel comfortable with—it is sometimes interesting to compare different translations.

To prepare for a session you should:

• read through the main passage(s) for the session

• read through the study notes and think about how you might approach the questions

• think of the people in the group. How familiar are they with the passage and what might their questions be? Keep in mind that you are not so much looking for 'right' answers but are working through the possible meaning together

• look up the leader's notes and note any materials you might need

• read through the 'Overview' and 'Verse-by-verse' notes. They will help you to grow in your own understanding

• think about the aims of the study session and how they will work with your group

• pray for your group members and for the group's time together

There is a reading list at the back in case you want to look up things out of personal interest. It is not required reading!

How do I lead a study group?

It may be that you have never led a small group Bible study before. Or you may be an old hand at it. Whatever your experience of small group Bible study may be, here are some hints and suggestions for leading your group through this particular material.

Discussion and exploration...

First and foremost, small groups function best as discussion and exploration groups. They are not really a place where the leader—or anyone else—should expect to tell others what to believe or what to think. Of course, there will always be times when group members need to be guided and focused in their exploration. But, nevertheless, these are discussion and exploration groups, and certainly not the place for anyone to indulge themselves in sermons, diatribes or monologues. When discussion dries up and the discussion feels a little stilted, it can be very tempting for leaders to jump in and talk too much. In the long run, it is best to resist this temptation, compelling though it is. If conversation dies, it's not the end of the world—you can always move on to another point! Discussion points are indicated in the Study notes by the faces icon.

Feeling safe to ask questions...

You should expect very little of the study material to be able to be answered by a direct or one-word answer. Small groups are places where people should feel free to speak their thoughts and their feelings and to open their hearts to others without being thought 'wrong' or 'unsound'. The questions are there to encourage discussion and exploration, not to provide pat 'answers'. People don't tend to grow by having their prejudices massaged and their assumptions confirmed!

Guiding and encouraging discussion...

'How long should I let discussion run on?' There is a tension here. On the one hand, good discussion is valuable, and shouldn't be unduly stifled by the leader. If a particular part of the study seems to 'catch fire', or to raise interesting questions for the group, you may well need to stick with it and let discussion develop. Sometimes it is best simply to 'go with the flow'. On the other hand, it is a pity to let 'red herrings' take up the time, so that you only get part of the way through the material. These study guides are not just a clutch of questions, thrown together at random. They tend to have an inbuilt momentum. Quite often, the 'guts' of the study are to be found towards the end of the session, and need to be got to if members are to benefit fully from the material. This is true throughout. *You will find there are key questions highlighted in bold italic in the study notes*, and the reflections and times of sharing personal feelings and reactions are always important.

The leader's role...

So, what is a leader's role? Not to preach; not to provide 'the answers'; but to facilitate and encourage discussion and reflection. Some of these studies invite group members to offer thoughts and insights from their own life experiences. People can feel very vulnerable when they attempt this. So part of a leader's task is to help members feel secure enough to share appropriately in the life of the group.

Worship and prayer...

'Should our group worship and pray together?' Ideally, yes. Some groups take to this more easily than others. This material is designed engage the whole person, to warm the heart as well as to stimulate thinking. There will be opportunities for sharing, for prayer, for silent meditation. The studies may invite people to speak, to look and to taste. Do encourage members to participate in this; but do also be aware of your group members' individual needs and expectations. People have very different temperaments; they tend to come from rather different backgrounds and church traditions; and they often have very different experiences of discussion, prayer and worship. The secret is invariably: don't impose, rather encourage.

Seven Signs in John's Gospel

1 Study notes: John
Introduction

What's in a sign? These studies are about seven 'signs' which John uses in his Gospel to point to some particular truths about Jesus.

As we work through them, we will find that these 'signs' often involve very...

VISIBLE   **TANGIBLE**   **MATERIAL**

things, like water, wine, bread and fish, mud and spit, which suggest a truth about Jesus. These truths about Jesus may not be as obvious as these everyday things—but they are still just as real.

Or they may involve miraculous events, like healings or raisings from the dead. These miracles, John tells us, have a very...

VISIBLE   **TANGIBLE**   **MATERIAL**

effect on people around Jesus. But they also point to something deeper, but just as real, about Jesus himself.

But these 'signs' aren't just meant to give you something to think about. Their purpose is to get the reader to *do something*. What that 'something to do' is will become clearer in the very first study.

But first... a quick exercise for you to do!

 Signposts exercise

Take a sheet of paper and a pen each. Design an attractive poster-style signpost to your church, to be placed somewhere where it will easily be seen by people who pass by.

Show your drawings to each other.

Discuss three things:

• What does this signpost *point to*?

• What is the signpost meant to *tell* a passer-by?

• What do you hope somebody might *do* on seeing the sign?

Keep these three things—point to, tell, do—in mind for the studies ahead.

John 2:1–11

Water into wine

This study focuses on the first 'sign' that John recounts. Read through it, and work through the discussion points that follow.

A puzzling reaction

Verses 4 and 5 aren't easy. Discuss any issues that you find problematic here.

What does Jesus mean by 'my hour has not yet come' (NRSV)? What is 'my hour' likely to refer to?

A huge quantity of water

Look at verse 6. The stone jars were for ritual hand-washing before meals. These rituals were important for many Jews of Jesus' day. Read the description of this in Mark 7:1–8.

Each jar held 20 to 30 gallons (100 to 150 litres). Calculate how many pints or litres of water there were in the six jars.

Read verses 7 and 8. Note how the jars were filled up to the brim. This huge quantity of water was about to be turned into wine.

The brim-full jars of water could be seen as a picture of the rituals of Jewish Law. Discuss for a moment if the 'sign' of brim-full jars of water turned into wine suggests that the Old Testament Law has been set aside, overturned, or brought to 'fulfilment' in Jesus. If so, what might this mean? Look up Matthew 5:17.

John's aim is not to stress the doing of the miracle. It is recounted in only four words in the Greek: 'the water-become-wine' (verse 9). Instead, he concentrates on the fact of vast quantities of water turned into huge amounts of wine. Why so much wine? Try and imagine, with the help of bottles on the table, the sort of quantities involved. Share any ideas this brings to mind.

Good quality wine

Read verses 8 to 10. Appreciate the humour there! The stress is on the last phrase: 'but you have kept the good wine until now!' (NRSV). The wine isn't just plentiful—it is *good* wine!

Read Amos 9:13–14. What thoughts and images does Amos' picture of wine suggest to you?

Think about the words 'until now' in verse 10. What do they mean? Might they have a connection with Jesus' words about his 'hour' in verse 4, and, if so, what is that connection?

The glory of Jesus

Read verse 11. By doing this sign, Jesus revealed his glory. What does his 'glory' signify? Read John 17:1 and 5. Jesus' glory was made complete in his death and resurrection. Think of the signpost you made earlier. It *pointed to* something. Who does the sign of water-into-wine point to?

The signpost you made also *told* people something about the church. What does the sign of water-into-wine tell you about Jesus?

The signpost you drew earlier didn't only point to the church and tell people where it was—it was meant to *influence* the people who saw it. How did this sign of water-into-wine affect the disciples?

Tasting and reflecting

If everyone agrees, do the following exercise.

Each taste some of the water; talk about what it tastes like.

Taste the wine (or other drink) together. Talk about what it tastes like. Compare the taste of the water and the wine. Talk together about the richness and abundance of God's mercy and blessing in Jesus, and about your response to him.

How does this sign of water-into-wine affect you? How might it deepen and enrich your relationship with God? Discuss this together. Use your imagination.

Have someone read Amos 9:13–14 again out loud. Use it as a stimulus for prayer and thanksgiving.

GROWTH POINTS

2 Healing an official's son

In this passage John recounts a healing which has a deeper significance. Read the passage and then work through the following discussion points.

Life

This passage is about death and life. In the presence of Jesus, which has the upper hand—death or life?

Read John 1:4. In our passage, Jesus restores someone to life. What else can be said about Jesus?

Read John 3:36. When and how can we have 'eternal life', and what do you think it is?

Read John 10:10. The word for 'abundantly' comes from the Greek 'to overflow'. What links does this suggest with what we discovered last session? What does this tell us about what eternal life is like?

Read the first part of John 4:46. Jesus wants us to link this 'sign' with the 'sign' we looked at last time. How does he achieve this? Why is he keen to make those connections clear to us?

Eternal life

What does the offer of eternal life now and in abundance mean for you at this moment? Discuss together ways in which you could enjoy today more of the abundance of eternal life in your walk with God.

Faith

Look at verse 48. Jesus is criticizing those who wonder at his miracles but don't see anything deeper in them. For John, this attitude amounts to shallow sensation-seeking. In verse 45 Jesus has hinted that the Galileans responded in this way: they *welcomed* him because of his miracles, but, unlike the non-Jewish Samaritans (verse 39), they didn't *believe* in him.

Read verses 46 and 47. The official requested Jesus to go and heal his son. He has come sixteen miles to do this. What was his probable attitude to Jesus at this point? Does he believe in Jesus, like the Samaritans? Or is he sensation-seeking, like the Jews? Or somewhere in between? How would you describe what he is thinking and feeling?

Read verses 49 and 50. The official is more insistent. Jesus responds with assurance. Read 1 Kings 17:23. There Elijah tells the widow 'See, your son lives.' What is different about John 4:50? What response do Jesus' words draw out of the official?

The official believed Jesus' word. He had the *beginnings* of faith, but not yet faith in *Jesus himself*. Discuss the difference. Write down 'The beginnings of faith' at the top of a sheet of paper. Look at verses 51 to 53. Once the miracle was confirmed, the official and his household 'believed'. They came to faith in Jesus. They needed the fulfilment of Jesus' promise to come to a real faith in him. All the same, they did come to see the truth about Jesus which lay behind the 'sign'. Write down 'A more developed faith' lower down the sheet of paper.

Personal reflection

Think back into your past and consider how the beginnings of faith and a more developed faith have been part of your experience. Write down on the sheet times and events which reflect these stages for you. You won't be asked to share what you write, unless you want to.

Where are you now on this journey of faith? Is there scope for your faith to be deepened still further? In what ways? How does this 'sign' of Jesus the life-giver deepen your faith?

Read Psalm 36:7–9 aloud slowly, with pauses for meditation. Pray for one another about any particular issues that have arisen as a result of this study.

GROWTH POINTS

3 John 5:1–24
Healing a sick man

Last time we looked at life and faith. This time we are concentrating more on the life Jesus gives as a gift. Read the passage and then work through the questions that follow.

The sick man

What was this man like and do you think that he was a particularly deserving case for healing by Jesus (see particularly verses 11, 15 and 16)?

What did the man think Jesus was offering to do and where did he expect his healing to come from?

Why do you think Jesus offered to make him well?

Jesus commands him, and at once the man is healed. John stresses this 'at once'. The healing happened suddenly. Jesus did it without the man going anywhere near the water!

The Jewish authorities

According to John, how did the Jewish authorities react to the healing and why did they react in this way?

How did *they* think God blesses a person?

The 'sign'

The sick man thought he would be healed if he managed to get into the water. The Jewish authorities thought you got good things from God if you kept to the rules. They were both wrong. Healing came to the sick man as a *gift*. Jesus healed him because he wanted to.

Read John 5:19–21. Though John doesn't call this healing a 'sign', we are meant to understand it that way. The healing of the man points to a deeper truth. Jesus says the Father will show the Son 'greater works than these'. 'These' works are the miracles Jesus has already done.

What are the 'greater works than these'?

Read verse 21 again: The Son gives life to anyone he chooses

Responding in prayer

Take a piece of paper each.

Write down anything in your life where you act like the sick man, looking elsewhere than Jesus for help.

Write down anything in your life where you are like the Jewish authorities, looking for life in rule-keeping.

If you feel you can, share some of these things together.

In verse 24 to whom does Jesus choose to give life?

Tear up the sheet of paper and put the pieces in the bin provided. Ask God to take these things away from you. (The bits of paper will be thrown away afterwards without being read!)

Read Psalm 85 together, meditatively, as in prayer. Perhaps one member of the group could read whilst others attentively listen. Mull over the words. Pick up some of the phrases in the psalm—verses 10 or 12, for example—and use them in prayer. Allow this to turn to wider prayer, of adoration and petition.

If you want, finish with this prayer:

> Thank you, Lord Jesus, life-giver,
> that you give us eternal life
> because you choose to.
> Give us life, we pray. Amen.

GROWTH POINTS

4 John 6:16–21
Walking on the water

John writes his account of Jesus walking on the water very starkly.
Read the passage and then think about the following aspects.

The disciples

 It was now dark (verse 17). Read John 1:5 and 13:30. What do you think the idea of darkness suggests or signifies in John's Gospel?

The Greek text says that Jesus had not yet come close to them (verse 17). He was still far away from them. The sea rose and a strong wind was blowing (verse 18). Though the disciples were experienced fishermen, Jews of Jesus' time were not generally fond of the sea. To them it was the abode of chaos, of all that God is not. Read Job 38:8–11 and/or Revelation 13:1 as an example of what the sea signified to them. So it was dark, the sea was rough, and Jesus was far away. How do you imagine the disciples felt at this moment?

Sharing our experience

 Each jot down on a piece of paper about a time in your life when you have felt that all was dark, that everything was chaotic, and that help and support was far away. That time might be in the past, or it might be a present experience.

If you feel able, share some of this together.

Jesus

 The disciples then saw Jesus walking on the water and coming close. What does the idea of walking on the water suggest to you? Who has power over what?

What does the idea of Jesus coming close suggest to you? Why does Jesus come close to his disciples?

Jesus has power over the elements. He has mastery and dominion over them. But he also wants to be close to individual human beings.

The disciples again

The disciples were frightened (verse19). Why did they react like this? What action could they have taken out of fear?

Read verses 20 and 21. Jesus speaks; his words calm their fear; and they willingly receive him into the boat.

Look again at what you have jotted down. In this story, Jesus, master of the elements, comes close to his disciples at a difficult time. Though fearful of him, they welcome him. What might this suggest to you about the time of difficulty you went through or are going through? If you feel able, talk about this together.

How John sees it

But how is this walking-on-water a 'sign'? John was writing his Gospel after Jesus' death and resurrection had taken place. So he could write and shape his Gospel with those events in mind.

Read John 1:1 and 20:28. John believed Jesus to be God. Next time we will see that Jesus says seven times 'I am...' in John's Gospel. Read verse 20. The Greek for 'it is I' can also mean 'I am'.

Read Exodus 3:13–15. God reveals his name to Moses as 'I am'.

Read John 8:58 and 59. In these verses, by saying 'I am' Jesus claims to be divine. According to John, the Jewish authorities knew it—and tried to stone him.

So John sees this story of walking-on-water as a hint to Jesus' divinity. He takes Jesus' simple words—'It is I'—and uses them to express a deeper truth: Jesus is God become man.

The sign

So to whom does this 'sign' point? What does it say about him? What does this 'sign' ask the reader to do? How are you going to respond to it?

Read Isaiah 43:1–2 out loud and allow time for silent meditation. Pray for any you know who are experiencing difficult times just now.

GROWTH POINTS

5 John 6:1–14
Feeding a large crowd

Read John 6:1–14. This is a familiar story, found in all four Gospels. But we are concentrating on one particularly significant aspect of the story—how John uses the feeding of the crowd as a visual aid to Jesus' revealing of himself as 'the bread of life'.

The setting

Why (verse 4) does John bother to mention that Jesus fed the crowd at Passover time? What would that make his Jewish readers think of? Read 6:31 and 32 to sharpen these ideas up.

Why does John mention (verse 3) that Jesus climbed a mountain? Who might that put his Jewish readers in mind of? (We will return to this later).

Why do you think people were following Jesus?

The 'sign'

Jesus gave thanks and distributed the bread (verse 11). Actually, the disciples probably handed it around to the huge number of people there. So why does John stress that the bread came from *Jesus*? What is he trying to tell his readers about Jesus?

Why does he note that there was plenty left over (verse 12)?

Why twelve basketsful left over? Who had Jesus come for?

Read verses 26–40. The bread is an important sign, and Jesus takes time to explain it. The people's attention had been on what was happening in their lives and on their immediate daily concerns—on miracles (verse 2); food (verse 26), and on victory over the Roman occupiers (verse 15). They wanted their needs met *immediately*, even if that meant only *temporarily*. Like manna in the wilderness (verse 31)—immediate, but only temporary. What were the people's real needs and how could they be met?

Manna fills the stomach and satisfies physical hunger. But what is the deeper, more lasting way in which Jesus satisfies? Reread verse 35.

Summary

The bread which fed the crowd is a sign. It points to Jesus. Jesus is the bread of life. What does this mean?

The bread also tells us that Jesus can satisfy our hunger and thirst. What does this mean?

As we have seen, John's 'signs' are there to draw a response out of us. What is your response to this 'sign'? How has receiving Jesus, the bread of life, affected your life? Is there room for you to receive more of him? In what ways? How might doing that affect you?

Reflecting on Jesus, the bread of life

If you have a display of bread, use it quietly to consider the idea of Jesus as the bread of life. Meditate on this. Praise and thank Jesus for being the bread of life. Acknowledge your hunger and your thirst. Offer them to him. Thank God for food and nourishment. Thank him that Jesus is the true bread of life and that we do not need to hunger and thirst.

Pass the bread around and share it quietly together.

GROWTH POINTS

6 John 9:1–41
Healing a blind man

Here John recounts a further healing, one which provides a variety of responses to him. Read the passage, and work through the discussion points below.

The blind man healed

There are various reasons why Jesus may have used saliva (verse 6). Discuss this, briefly, if you wish.

Look at the following passages in John's Gospel: 3:17, 3:34, 5:36, and 20:21. Who, in John's view, is Jesus? See if you can find other passages in John's Gospel where Jesus is referred to in the same way.

Now look back at John 9:7. John makes a point of telling us what 'Siloam' means. It means 'Sent', or 'the Sent One'. With this in mind, what, for John, is the man really doing in going to wash in the pool? What is this action a picture of? Who—in effect—is the man going to, to be healed?

In verse 5, what does Jesus say he is? Read John 1:9: who is Jesus? Not only does the blind man go to Jesus, the Sent One. He also goes to Jesus, the Light of the World, for healing, and receives his sight.

The man's reaction

This man's understanding of what Jesus did and who Jesus was developed during the course of this story. Read verses 17, 25, 31 and 35–38 in particular to see this. At first, who does he think Jesus is? Who does he end up thinking Jesus is? And what response does he make?

The Pharisees' reaction

Read verse 16. The Pharisees were divided. What did the two groups think? Was either group right, and why?

By verse 24, the Pharisees seem to have sorted out their differences. Which view of Jesus do they settle for? Read Isaiah 8:6. Siloam (or Shiloah) again! How could this prophecy relate to the Pharisees in this story? What is John hinting about them?

What the light does

The healing of the blind man is a 'sign'. It is a picture of Jesus, light of the world, giving light to a dark world, healing to a blind world. Yet the man had to respond first! Read verse 39. The light which Jesus brings judges people. The Greek for 'judgment' means a dividing of humanity on the basis of our *response* to Jesus. What does this verse tell us about human responses to Jesus? What does it tell us about the response of the Pharisees, and of the blind man? Who, in this story, is truly blind?

Jesus' response to the Pharisees

Read verse 40. The Pharisees can't believe that Jesus thinks they are blind! After all, they know and practise the Law of Moses, don't they!

Read verse 41. What does Jesus mean by 'if you were blind'? What does he mean by 'now that you say, "We see"'? In what way is their attitude or *response* to him important?

What is Jesus' final word here to the Pharisees?

Jesus' response to the man

Read verse 34. The Pharisees threw out the man. Read John 6:37. The Greek for 'drive away' is exactly the same as 'throw out'. Read 9:35. The man had come to Jesus, the Sent One, the Light of the World, and received his sight. The Pharisees threw him out. Jesus, though, sought him out, because he never drives away anyone who comes to him.

Sharing our own responses

Ponder the fate of these Pharisees, who thought they could see and ended up blinded by Jesus' light.

Consider the destiny of the man, who knew he was blind and was brought to sight.

Read John 12:46. What is your response to Jesus, the light of the world? Have you acknowledged your 'blindness' to him, and asked him for 'sight'?

Are there still areas where you think you can 'see' without Jesus' help? If so, offer them to God.

Take time as a group to worship Jesus, as the man did.

GROWTH POINTS

7 John 11:1–45
Raising Lazarus

This account has been called the climax of all Jesus' signs in John's Gospel. Read the passsage, and consider the questions which follow.

Why did Lazarus die? (John 11:1–6)

What, according to John, was the purpose of Lazarus' illness?

Read John 9:3, from last time you met. What, according to John, was the purpose of the blind man's disability?

How do you feel about the idea of God using illness and death to further his purposes? How well or badly does this idea gel with modern ideas of morality and human freedom?

Read verse 33. If illness and death can, at times, be turned to God's good purposes, does it necessarily mean that these aspects of human experience are themselves good?

Does God always use illness and death for his glory? Are illness and death ever simply bad? What do your personal experiences of illness and bereavement contribute to this discussion?

Jesus and Lazarus (John 11:7–18)

Where did Lazarus die? Where did Jesus (eventually) go to raise him? What happened to Jesus later near the same city?

Note the disciples' protests in verse 8 and Thomas' comment in verse 16. What does Thomas believe to be the likely outcome of this journey? Read John 11:45–53 and 13:1. Is he right or wrong? But what doesn't he yet understand at all about Jesus' plans?

In this story John closely links Lazarus' death and raising with Jesus' death and resurrection. What is Lazarus' death and raising a 'sign' of? What does it point us forward to? Why?

Jesus and Martha (John 11:19–45)

Because this is a long passage, we're going to concentrate on one aspect—Jesus' dealings with Martha. We meet her properly in verses 20–22. What do you think Martha was thinking and feeling about

Lazarus' death? About Jesus' delay? About what Jesus might do? What did she say to Jesus? What feelings lay behind her words?

Verse 23: How did Jesus respond to what she said? Look back to verses 11–13. There, Jesus had been deliberately vague, saying at first that Lazarus had simply fallen asleep. In what way was he deliberately vague with Martha? Why do you think he did this?

Verse 24: Martha thought Jesus was referring to the resurrection of the dead on the day of judgment. The Pharisees held this doctrine. No doubt some of them held it as a general, detached belief. It was the only solace Martha could find in her brother's death. Are there any doctrines we hold like this? Do we have any general, detached beliefs that don't really connect with our daily life and experiences, which don't really address the difficulties and problems we face? What are they?

Note Jesus' response. 'I am'. Not 'there will be...' or 'we believe in...' but 'I am'. Jesus sharpened up her faith. He challenged her understanding.

Verse 26: What did Jesus ask of Martha here? Why?

Note what Jesus was doing. He was moving her on from a general, detached acceptance of an idea to real, personal faith and trust in him.

Verse 27: What response did Martha make?

Jesus and us

 Jesus said Lazarus' death was to glorify him. He used it to challenge Martha and to move her on from *a fairly general detached acceptance of an idea* to *a more specific personal trust in Jesus as Lord*.

Even when we are at a loss, as Martha was, detached acceptance of ideas about Jesus is not enough. We are called to personal trust in him.

 *Read verses 25–27 again. In what areas could I move further from detached acceptance of ideas about God to deeper personal trust in Jesus as God's Anointed One (Messiah), Lord and Son of God? How might that affect who I am and what I do?*

Read Colossians 2:6–7 and pray about areas in your own life and in the life of your church in the light of this passage.

 GROWTH POINTS

8 Final session
Drawing it all together

Signposts exercise

Make paper or cardboard posters on the sheets of A3 paper, one for each session you have done. Each should have the name of the sign ('Water-into-wine', etc) at the top. Divide each poster into two sections by a line. One section should have 'tells us that Jesus...' at the top. The other section should have 'our response...' at the top.

Look at the posters and decide together what each 'sign' you have studied *tells you* about Jesus. Don't just say, for example, 'Jesus is the light of the world' and tick that one off! Really talk together about what that means. Fill in the relevant part of the poster with your ideas.

Decide together how life is going to be different for you, individually or as a group, as a result of studying this particular 'sign'. *This is the most important part of the exercise: John's 'signs' demand a response!* Fill in the relevant part of the poster with your thoughts.

Prayer and worship

Read Psalm 36:7–9.

How many of the themes we have studied are contained in these verses?

Use each line of the psalm passage as an introduction to prayer. Allow some silence after each line, to give an opportunity for people to be quiet together, or for them to pray out loud. Pray or be quiet together for as long as it takes.

When you have finished, why not take some time to relax together? You will have earned it!

1 Leader's notes: John 2:1–11
Water into Wine

Aims

• For members to understand more of how this 'sign', or picture, of good wine manifests Jesus' glory and splendour as God's chosen one.

• For their faith in him to be increased and deepened.

Introduction to 'Seven Signs in John's Gospel'

Welcome to this series of small-group Bible studies on 'Seven Signs in John's Gospel'. These studies are offered to you as a resource. They have been written to provide a stimulating and imaginative way in to this part of John's Gospel. They are designed to help us answer the twin questions: 'Who does John say Jesus is?' and 'What does this mean for us and for others today?' If this material helps you and your group members understand and experience the love and the rule of Jesus Christ in your lives in some new or deeper way, then it will have succeeded in its aims.

Materials required for this session

• Paper and pencils

• A pint milk bottle full of water

• A bottle of wine (see 'Overview' below)

NB There are *two double pages* for this week's study notes, including the introduction.

Overview

The bottles should be placed on a coffee table or similar, where everyone can see them, before the meeting starts. They will be used during the meeting as a way to appreciate the force and power of John's sign of water-into-wine.

This will require sensitivity from the study leader(s). You will need to sort out before the meeting starts what you are going to do with the water and wine. Be sensitive to any non-drinkers among you. If appropriate, some low- or non-alcoholic wine could be used alongside the wine for non-drinkers.

Verse-by-verse

The study notes and leader's notes quote NRSV, unless stated otherwise.

1 In Jewish custom of the time, weddings were a time of great celebration, lasting as long as a week. Wedding presents were customary, and often demanded from the guests by right! In return, the groom provided the hospitality, and the wine flowed freely. So to run out of wine would cause intolerable shame and embarrassment.

3 What was Mary expecting of Jesus? Since this is the first of the 'signs' John recounts, we are probably not supposed to think she was expecting a miracle. On the other hand, Mary may have already been widowed by now (see Mark 6:3) and used to placing some reliance on her son's resourcefulness. Whatever, John uses Mary's comment

28

as a way of addressing Jesus with the problem of the lack of wine.

4 'Woman': in Greek, not the usual term for a son to use to his mother. A little abrupt, perhaps, but not as rude as 'woman' in English. 'Dear woman' might be a better translation.

'What have you to do with me?': the Hebrew phrase underlying this comment is a flexible one. Here, it probably means something more like 'why do you involve me?'.

'My hour': does this refer to the time when Jesus was to begin to reveal himself by signs, or the time when he was to be glorified through his death, resurrection and exaltation? John tends to see Jesus' earthly ministry as of a piece with his death, resurrection and exaltation. He sees them as continuous, like a seamless garment. Jesus' life anticipates his death, which gives rise to his resurrection. It is probable that John is focusing here on the *completion* of his earthly work in his death and resurrection. Matthew uses the picture of a wedding (Matthew 22:1–4; 25:1–13) to depict the consummation of the age of the Messiah. This 'sign' of good wine is probably to be understood as an enacted picture of the new reality brought to completion by the whole of Jesus' earthly life. 'My hour' probably refers more, then, to the completion of that work.

2 Healing an official's son

Aims

• For members to understand how this 'sign' of life represents and symbolizes eternal life, available now.

• For them to understand how this 'sign' of life confirms the beginnings of faith, calls forth greater faith and deepens it, leading the believer to Jesus.

• For them to consider the depth of their faith and allow that faith to be deepened by this 'sign' of life.

Materials required for this session

• Paper and pencils

Life

The study notes ask people to cross-refer to John 1:4. John's second sign isn't just a story about a young man brought back to life—though it is that. It's not even just a story about a miracle which Jesus performed—though it is that also. It is a pointer to the real life that is in Jesus—eternal life. Part of the aim of this study is to explore what it means to have eternal life.

The study notes also refer across to John 3:36, and ask people to consider when, according to John, eternal life starts—now, or in the future? The *revivification* of a young man does not, of course, amount to 'new life' in the *resurrection* sense of that term. But John does appear to use it as a 'sign' to signify the eternal life which is offered by Jesus and which is indeed in him. The official's son was granted life by Jesus—with immediate effect. Eternal life is not just for the future—according to John, it can start now.

Faith

John's Gospel describes faith as a developing process. Sensation-seeking (the Jews' approach, so John says), belief in Jesus' word (the official's position at the outset) and fuller faith (the official's later stance) represent different stages in the process of faith. John criticizes sensation-seeking, but is much more positive about the other two.

This 'sign' of life has two aspects. First, Jesus grants it in response to the faith the official had. Secondly, the 'sign' itself helped to deepen the official's faith. Thus the twin issues of *life* and *faith* are interrelated in this story.

Verse-by-verse

44 In the other Gospels, the term for Jesus' 'own country' means his home town, Nazareth. Here it probably means the Jewish areas of Galilee and Judea, as opposed to Samaria. Jesus has just come from Samaria, where many have believed in him (4:39–42). Jesus' welcome in Jewish territory will be rather different, based more on his ability to perform spectacular *miracles* rather than on *who he is*. Samaritans were greatly despised by Jews, so John's recollection of the proverb in verse 44 is highly ironic.

46 'an official': probably a senior official of the court of the tetrarch Herod Antipas, son of Herod the Great.

The back-reference noted in the study notes is sometimes called 'recapitulation'. Its purpose is to show that John is exploring, through this second 'sign', another facet of Jesus' identity. We are meant to put both 'signs' together and begin to build up a picture of Jesus' identity of significance.

48 John records the words 'signs and wonders' here. It isn't used positively. There is an important contrast here. On the one hand, Jesus' miracles as 'signs' are viewed as material pointers towards deep theological truths about Jesus. On the other hand, as 'signs and wonders' they can be taken simply at face-value. But shallow reliance on them alone cannot amount to life-giving faith. Jesus' miraculous acts have, for John, a deeper purpose than their face-value effect: to call forth faith out of those who witnessed them and out of the reader of John's Gospel. The commentator Schnackenburg (page 476) puts it like this: 'There is a way of seeing signs that [John's] Jesus desires and approves of. But if the "signs" are not grasped in faith, they are nothing but outward miracles, and this is what the evangelist expresses in the phrase "signs and wonders"'.

50–53 John uses the verb 'to believe' in different ways, to describe different points along the spectrum of faith. See the comments above for an expansion of this point.

The New Testament contains various shades of understanding as to the 'last things'. John's view of the 'last things' (his 'eschatology') is quite strongly 'realized'. In other words, his emphasis is that eternal life is, to a large measure, available here and now to the believer. The writers of the other Gospels, and Paul offer a slightly different emphasis. They agree that eternal life is available now, but also stress that there is greater depth and richness of life to come at the end of things. John does not deny this, but concentrates more on the here-and-now availability of eternal life. These various emphases are complementary, not contradictory.

3
John 5:1–24
Healing a sick man

Aims

• For group members to understand this miracle of healing as something given by Jesus.

• For them to see this 'sign' of healing as a pointer to God's gift of life in Jesus.

• For them to reaffirm their belief in Jesus as life-giver.

Materials required for this session

• Sheets of paper

• Pencils

• A waste paper basket.

Overview

This healing, its effects, and the discourse following are connected, as the study shows. The miracle itself can be approached on at least two levels:
• as a miracle seen as an event in itself

• as a 'sign' pointing to how Jesus gives life to believers.

This study approaches the material primarily at the second level, that of the miracle as a 'sign' pointing to something else.

Therefore:

• It would be inappropriate to allow discussion to get bogged down in issues of healing

• Though the miracle of healing points to truths about eternal life, healing and eternal life are not identical issues and so cannot be totally superimposed on each other. For example, John implies that the sick man was healed even though he seems to have put no real trust in Jesus. On the other hand, eternal life as a gift does, for John, depend on faith (for example, 5:24). Care needs to be taken, then, as to how the issues of healing and eternal life are related. It would be best to concentrate on the idea of gift; and to start talking about faith only at the point of application at the end of the study. After all, John has Jesus bring in the question of faith only when developing the issue of eternal life towards the end of the passage.

Verse-by-verse

1   It isn't certain which of the three Jewish pilgrim festivals of Deuteronomy 16—Passover, Weeks or Tabernacles—is referred to here. The fact that John doesn't specify suggests that the identity of the feast contributes nothing to his account.

2   The pool may have been called Bethzatha, 'house of olives'. More likely it was called Bethesda, which may mean either 'house of mercy' or 'house of outpouring'. It is in the north-east part of Jerusalem, near the present church of St Anne. John doesn't translate the name into Greek, so its meaning may well be unimportant for him here. Archaeology suggests that the pool was once associated with the pagan cult of healing presided over by the god Aesculapius.

The nature of its water supply meant that, every so often, the waters of the pool were disturbed. This gave rise to the notion that the first person into the waters when they were disturbed would be healed.

3   Verses 3b and 4 (in the margin) are probably not original, but a later gloss to explain verse 7.

4 John 6:16–21
Walking on water

Aims

• To understand the significance of John's use of dark/ chaos/ Jesus' absence contrasted with Jesus' presence.

• To appreciate Jesus' power and yet his concern for the individual.

• To let these things speak to group members through exploration of a time of difficulty in their own lives.

Materials required for this session

• Paper and pencils

NB This week you might like to ask group members to bring along items for next week's session—and decide now if you need to say anything this week.

Overview

Modern biblical scholarship demonstrates that the Gospel writers weren't just writing stories or even simply history. They were writing for a purpose, and each of them had a rather different purpose. There are reasons and judgments behind the way they frame what they write and behind the order they put things in.

This account of the walking on the water seems much starker and rough-hewn than its parallels in Matthew 14 and Mark 6. The reasons John includes it in his Gospel are very different from their reasons for doing so. For instance, Matthew and Mark are interested in the disciples' difficulties on the lake and Jesus stilling of the storm. John is not much interested in the first and not at all in the second of these ideas. The study material gives a fair indication of John's theological interests here.

One consequence of this is that it would be for the best to avoid comparing Gospel accounts of this miracle or filling in the gaps in one account from another. That would simply blur an appreciation of what John is trying to do.

Verse-by-verse

20 John places this account between the multiplication of the bread—which we look at next time—and Jesus' explanation of that 'sign' in terms of 'I am the bread of life', the first of the seven 'I am' sayings. The 'I am/ it is I' of verse 20 (see the last part of the study notes) arguably sets the scene for all seven of those sayings. John interprets this 'I am/ it is I' as a pointer to Jesus' divinity. In this context, all seven 'I am' sayings become, for John, implicit claims to Jesus' divinity.

21 Commentators are divided as to whether the 'immediately the boat was at the land...' is meant to describe a further miracle. This is at least possible, but that issue doesn't actually take the aim of this session any further.

5 Feeding a large crowd

John 6:1–14

Aims:

• To explore the idea of Jesus as the bread of life by means of discussion, meditation and prayer, through study, a display and a simple act of sharing bread.

• To consider what it may mean for group members that Jesus is the bread of life, and to respond accordingly.

Materials required for this session

• Loaf of bread and/or rolls.

• Pictures of wheat/bread/ harvesting.

• Card with 'I am the bread of life' written clearly on it

Sharing bread together

Please note that the act of sharing bread at the end is a symbolic way of responding to Jesus' invitation in 6:35 to come to him. Understood this way it has nothing to do with the use of bread in the eucharist. John probably does not have the Lord's Supper directly in mind here. If you share some of the bread as the study notes suggest, it should be clear that this is not a eucharist in any way. A word of explanation at the time may also help allay any concerns here.

Display

You will need a loaf of bread (suitable for distribution) in a basket as the focus of a display on the theme of bread. This is to be an aid for meditation, so it needs to be visible to everyone from where they sit. Ideas for the display: pictures of bread/wheat/harvesting/milling; ears of wheat; flour; bread baking tins; bran; bread board and knife; card with the words 'I am the bread of life'; bread in all forms and sizes— why not ask each member to bring a loaf or roll?

Overview

It would be good to appreciate something of the structure of chapter 6 and the flow of its thought. The account of the walking on the water comes between the sign of the bread and fish and Jesus' words on 'I am the bread of life'. Though we are concentrating on the sign of the feeding, that sign and Jesus' words about bread in verses 25 to 40 are very much interlinked. Neither is complete without the other.

John's picture of Jesus progresses something like this:

Jesus gives the crowd a sign and satisfies their hunger by multiplying bread (1–13); he [the Son of Man] will give them food which 'endures for eternal life' (27); that food is the 'bread of God' which the Father gives (32) and which comes down from heaven and gives life to the world (33); Jesus is that bread, the bread of life (35).

The crowd's responses are as follows:

In reaction to the sign they see him as the 'prophet who is come into the world' (14). They have in mind Deuteronomy 18:15–19; yet they misinterpret Jesus as a political saviour (15); they are following Jesus because he satisfied their physical needs (26); despite having seen the multiplication of the bread, they demand a sign (30); Jesus criticizes them for having seen him and still not believing (36).

Jesus' words to the crowd are something like this:

Instead of looking for perishable food, they should be working for food that endures for eternal life (27); that work is to believe in Jesus (29); Jesus tells them to come to him and believe in him, the bread of life (35). If they do so, he will satisfy all their needs and give them eternal life (35, 40).

So there are at least three aspects to this passage:
• an exploration of who Jesus is and what his work is;

• repeated statements as to what people are to do in response to him, and what that will mean for them;

• an account of the crowd's failure to penetrate anywhere beneath the surface. They remain sensation-seekers and are unable to see the real meaning of Jesus or of the signs that point to him.

In this study we concentrate on:
• who Jesus is and what God's purposes in him are;

• what the right response to him is.

Verse-by-verse

1 'the other side': the east side of the Sea of Galilee.

2 We have had only one sign of healing so far, in chapter 5. But John is clearly selecting signs out of a larger number he knows about. See John 20:30.

3 Why does John trouble to record that Jesus and the disciples went up the mountain? We are probably meant to think of Moses at Sinai, and to reflect on how much greater than Moses Jesus is. This is especially likely since Jesus, the 'true bread from heaven', later compares himself with manna, which was also bread from heaven, but temporary and inferior: (31–33). *Moses* led the people through the wilderness to Sinai. They were fed and given water by God through his actions. Yet, in receiving *Jesus*, people need now never be hungry or thirsty (35).

4 Hence mention of the Passover. Here we are clearly meant to think about the manna in the wilderness: see verses 31–33.

9 It is possible that John (unlike the other Gospel writers) mentions *barley* loaves to put us in mind of the story of Elisha in 2 Kings 4:42–44, where he fed 100 people with 20 loaves of barley and 'had some left'.

11 Jesus gave thanks. There is much scholarly discussion whether John means to make a link with the eucharist. Most think not, or at least not directly.

John stresses that Jesus distributed the bread. Presumably he passed it out to the disciples to hand around. It's worth contrasting the different accounts here. Matthew 14:14 emphasizes that Jesus pitied the crowd and healed the ill. Mark 6:34 stresses that Jesus pitied them as sheep without a shepherd. But John isn't greatly interested in the crowd's particular needs. He stresses that the bread came from Jesus. *John's picture is not so much of a miracle done to satisfy need, but of a sign done to reveal who Jesus is—the life-giver.*

12 As with the water-into-wine, the doing of the miracle is very understated. We are not told how it was done. All we get to indicate a miracle are the words '... as much as they wanted' (11), 'When they were satisfied' (12) and the basketsful left over. We are meant to concentrate, not on the *miracle*, but on the *sign*.

The number 12 is significant. It refers to the twelve tribes of Israel. One commentator notes: 'the Lord has enough to supply the needs of the twelve tribes of Israel'—and more!

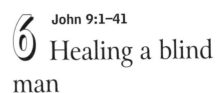

6 John 9:1–41
Healing a blind man

Aims

• For members to understand Jesus as 'the Sent One' and as the light of the world.

• For them to respond to Jesus, light of the world, by acknowledging their blindness and worshipping him.

Materials required for this session

None

Overview

The healing of the blind man is a sign pointing to Jesus, the Light of the World. The blind man comes to the Light of the World and sees. Paradoxically, those Pharisees who think they see, are truly blind, because they reject Jesus.

Verse-by-verse

2   The disciples assume that suffering is the result of specific sin. So do the Pharisees (34). But Jesus denies the close link they have made (3). In a general sense, surely, sin and suffering are connected: suffering is one of the consequences of human fallenness. But here the disciples try to make a much tighter link between this man's suffering and specific sins on his part or on the part of his forebears. The general witness of scripture doesn't support

this. In Deuteronomy there is doubt as to whether sins committed by earlier generations affect later ones. 5:9 suggests they do, but 24:16 provides that children should not be punished for their children's crimes, or vice versa. The prophets took up the idea that there was no responsibility across generations for sins committed: see Jeremiah 31:30; Ezekiel 18:1–4. The book of Job also supports this view.

4–5 Verse 4 includes the disciples in Jesus' work: 'we must do the works of him who sent me'. But do these 'works' refer to those done during Jesus' earthly ministry, or do they include later works by the disciples? In other words, when is the period of 'light' and that of 'night'? Here John is probably focusing on the pre-Easter work of Jesus and his followers. 'Day' is whilst Jesus is on earth; 'night' is once he has gone.

5 'I am the light of the world' is an important pointer here. Note the following:

The phrase picks up Jesus' words in 8:12, where the context is conflict with the authorities.

This 'I am' claim shows that this healing is a 'sign'. Giving the blind man sight becomes a picture of Jesus giving light to a dark world. The sign points to the fact that the work of the Father through Jesus is to shed light on those who live in darkness.

6 Why spittle and earth? Some think Jesus had in mind a reference to Genesis 2:7: just as humankind was made out of dust, so dust was used for this healing. This seems unlikely! Or spittle could communicate ritual impurity (Leviticus 15:8). Was Jesus turning a source of impurity into a means of blessing? This seems unlikely too: there seems no reason for this; and the authorities make no specific complaint over the use of saliva. More likely: saliva was thought to have healing properties—perhaps Jesus was simply using a practice frequently

adopted. Mark reports him as using spittle to heal in 7:33 and 8:23.

7 The pool of Siloam is on the slope of the old Jerusalem city hill. It is fed by the spring Gihon through the tunnel dug by Hezekiah before the attack of 701BC: see 2 Chronicles 32:30. In Hebrew, 'Siloam' can refer to the conduit (the 'sending forth') through which the water comes, or can mean 'sent'. In Isaiah 8:6 the Jews are pictured as refusing the waters of Shiloah; here, they refuse Jesus, the Sent One. So John sees this washing in Siloam as a symbolic cleansing and as an act of identification by the blind man with Jesus, the Sent One.

13 'the Pharisees': the man was taken to the local Pharisaic religious leaders for advice about the religious aspects of what had happened.

14 'the Sabbath': Jesus had broken Jewish regulations on probably three points: healing in a non-urgent case; making the mud paste by kneading; possibly, anointing the eyes.

15 The procedure of a first interrogation (15), enquiry of the parents (18) and a second interrogation (24) shows that this was a formal investigation. 'Give glory to God' (24) is a formula which put the witness under oath.

16 'from God' doesn't refer to where Jesus came from, but where he got his *authority* from. Some Pharisees couldn't accept that Jesus acted on God's behalf—how could he, if he was a law-breaker? Others thought he couldn't be a sinner if God had healed the man. Both were essentially wrong. The first group had a faulty understanding of the Law. As to the second, the doing of miracles doesn't of itself prove that the miracle worker comes 'from God'.

34 The Greek for 'and they threw him out' exactly parallels 6:37: 'whoever comes to me I will never drive away'.

Note the contrast: the Pharisees rejected the healed man, but Jesus will never reject anyone. This is why Jesus seeks the man out. The man is holding out for what he knows happened to him without full knowledge or understanding of Jesus, whom, after all, he has never seen! Jesus' purpose in finding him is to lead him to fuller faith.

38 In its original setting, it is probable that the man, in worshipping Jesus, meant to pay him homage as redeemer. He probably did not believe him to be God himself. But John definitely intends more than this in including the story. For John, Jesus is God, and John understands that the healed man is 'worshipping' better than he knew! One writer's comment is very revealing: 'the man has now become sighted in a double sense'!

39 Jesus' words show that he has come to turn things upside down. 'Those who do not see' are those who are in darkness and realize that this is so. After all, a blind person knows he is blind. They are to be given their sight. 'Those who see' are, for Jesus, those who *think* they can see, but in fact can't. The Pharisees think that the Law of Moses and the additional regulations tacked on to it enable them to see God as he is. But they can't. The irony is that they are unaware of their blindness. Paradoxically, when Jesus, the light of the world, comes, they turn away from him and are in a sense blinded by his light. What separates these people is their response to Jesus. *Those who know they need him are saved, but those who refuse to acknowledge that need are not.*

40 The Pharisees know Jesus means spiritual blindness. Their question assumes they think they have 20/20 vision.

41 Jesus' reply effectively means: 'if you realized you were blind...'

7

John 11:1–45

Raising Lazarus

Aims

• To help members move on from any *general*, detached beliefs about Jesus to deeper *personal* trust in him.

Materials required for this session

None.

Overview

One commentator calls this 'the climax of all Jesus' signs' in John's Gospel.

Verse-by-verse

3 'Lord': as they probably spoke Aramaic, the term used would have been 'rabbi'. This would acknowledge that Jesus was master and the sisters disciples, but it isn't in any way a confession of Jesus' divinity.

4 'This illness does not lead to death...': clearly Jesus doesn't mean that the illness isn't fatal. Rather he means that the ultimate outcome will not be Lazarus' death.
'It is for God's glory...': look back to 9:3, where the purpose of the man's blindness is said to be that God's work might be displayed in him.
But there is more to note here. To raise Lazarus, Jesus chose to go to Jerusalem. As 11:8 and 16 show, in going to Jerusalem Jesus is going to his death. In fact, the act of raising Lazarus precipitates the Sanhedrin action against him: verse 45f. So the death of Lazarus and his resuscitation is meant to make us think ahead to the death

and resurrection of Jesus. Jesus' glory is shown above all in his death and resurrection. So the raising of Lazarus from death, though totally different in kind to Jesus' resurrection, is meant to foreshadow those events recounted later in the Gospel.

8 'a short while ago' refers back to the attempted arrest of 10:39.

10 The NIV is unhelpful here. The last phrase of the verse should read: '... because the light is not in them'. Verse 9 talks literally of light. But this verse talks about it metaphorically: the light is the light of Jesus, within the believer.

15 'so that you may believe...': this adds to verse 4.

16 What thoughts may be behind Thomas' words? Probably devotion, determination, even courage. But also incomprehension: neither he nor the others understand that Jesus' death is part of the plan. This is a good example of *two layers of meaning* within the text: from our perspective, after the first Easter, the words are capable of another layer of meaning—a call to discipleship, to take up our cross and follow Jesus— which Thomas could not have intended. But John, of course, had both perspectives in mind when writing his Gospel.

17 The rabbis held the belief that the soul stayed in the tomb for three days after death. After that, once the body started to decompose, the soul left and death was from that point irreversible. That Lazarus was four days in the tomb is meant to stress the awesome character of the sign which follows.

23 Jesus' words are ambiguous. They could refer to the resurrection of the dead, which the Pharisees believed in. As such, they would be an attempt to console Martha. Martha interprets the words this way in verse 24.

25 Note the contrast between Martha's 'at the last day' and Jesus' words '*I am* the resurrection and the life'. With Jesus, the possibility of eternal life has become a present reality.

26 A complicated verse. Literally, '...will never die' reads '...will not die to eternity'. Verses 25 and 26 could be understood this way:

Belief:	One who believes in Jesus
Life:	will live
Death:	even though he must die physically.

Belief:	One who believes
Life:	and so lives
Death:	will not die for ever, but will live eternally.

So Jesus' words relate to three things: belief; eternal life in the present, as discussed in the second session; and what happens at the resurrection of the dead. Jesus says that, not only will those who believe in him be raised *at the last*, but they will have eternal life *now*.

33 'He was deeply moved in spirit' gives the wrong picture. Jesus wasn't just deeply moved; he was outraged and extremely angry. The Greek suggests he was snorting with anger and stirred up. Why? Probably not just at Lazarus' death. Probably not just at the mourning of the Jews: there is no suggestion they were acting hypocritically. It is more likely that his anger was provoked at the whole human condition of sinfulness and unbelief which leads to sickness, mortality and death.

8 Final session

Drawing it all together

Aims

• To return to the idea of signposts—to whom they point; what they tell us; and what they ask us to do.

• To help members consolidate what they have learnt about Jesus through John's use of signs.

• To help them make a response to Jesus on the basis of the signs John has used.

Materials required

• Sheets of A3 paper or card

• Two different coloured marker pens (for use in the two different sections of the posters)

Overview

At the beginning of the session the group makes seven posters, one for each of the signs. Each should have the name of the sign ('Water-into-wine', and so on) at the top. Divide each poster into two sections by a line. One section should have 'tells us that Jesus…' at the top. The other section should have 'our response…' at the top. Each section needs to be big enough for members to see from where they sit.

The idea is that members should be given the opportunity to recollect each sign study, to remind themselves of what the sign tells us about Jesus, and, most importantly, to bring together and articulate their responses to those signs. It is best to do this visually—the effect will be much more memorable.

The summary session finishes with a look at Psalm 36:7–9. This is because this passage brings together various themes we have studied over these sessions: abundance, life, light. It does this conveniently and poetically, and so is useful to round off the unit. A useful version is from the New Revised Standard Version of the Bible:

> *How precious is your steadfast love, O God!*
> *All people may take refuge in the shadow of your wings.*
> *They feast on the abundance of your house,*
> *and you give them to drink from the river of your delights.*
> *For with you is the fountain of life;*
> *in your light we see light.*

This may be a shorter session than usual. But don't worry. Just relax together.

Matthew's Gospel: A story about Jesus

1   *Introduction*

      Matthew 3:1–17   Preparation for ministry

2   *Matthew 9:1–17, 35–38*   Ministry and authority

3   *Matthew 11:1–6; 12:22–37*   Some responses to Jesus

4   *Matthew 16:21–17:9*   Passion and transfiguration

5   *Matthew 21:23–46*   A question of authority

6   *Matthew 26:57–68;*
      27:1–2, 11–31   Religious and political trial

7   *Matthew 28:1–20*   The great commission

1 Introduction

Some scholars believe that there are three distinct sections in Matthew's Gospel:

1 The preparation for Jesus (1:1—4:16)

2 The proclamation of Jesus (4:17—16:20)

3 The passion and resurrection of Jesus (16:21—28:20)

In these seven studies, we shall look at one passage from the first section, two from the second, and four from the third. Our aim is to see how these passages fit into this way of looking at the Gospel of Matthew—as well as to discover what we can learn from them for our own lives today.

It is as if Matthew has carefully crafted a story for us. Stories tend to have beginnings, middles and ends. The beginning gets us off to a good start, and introduces the characters. The middle develops the storyline. The end often provides a resolution to the story. Throughout, there tends to be a sense of progression or development.

A good story

 Brainstorm together: what are the ingredients of a good story? What makes a story gripping and enjoyable? What good stories have you read lately, and why did they hold your attention?

Matthew introduces the theme of each section of his Gospel in the first verse of that section. The material in that section then expands upon this introductory verse.

Look up 1:1, 4:17 and 16:21. Make a note of what these verses say in the chart below, under 'Heading'.

Each section develops into a climax, and each section builds upon the one before. So the Gospel progresses to its final resolution.

Look up 3:17, 16:16 and 27:54. Who is speaking in each case? What do they say about Jesus? Jot down what they say in the chart below, under the heading 'Climax'. Note particularly the words or titles they use of Jesus.

Section 1   1:1–4:16   **Title** The preparation of Jesus

Heading 1:1

Climax 3:17

Section 2   4:17–16:20   **Title** The proclamation of Jesus

Heading 4:17

Climax 16:16

Section 3   16:21–28:20   **Title** The passion and
resurrection of Jesus

Heading 16:21

Climax 27:54

Preparation for ministry

This chapter is part of the first section of Matthew's Gospel. It introduces us to **John the Baptist** and the **Pharisees** and the **Sadducees**. In it we also learn more about **Jesus**; and **God** himself. These are the key players in the story. Read the passage and then look at each of these in turn.

John the Baptist (Matthew 3:1–6)

 Matthew gives us some detail about John's appearance and location. Look at 2 Kings 1:8; Malachi 4:5; and Matthew 17:10–13. Who from Israel's past is John meant to represent?

 What was John's message? What did it mean? What is Matthew's purpose in recording this for us here?

John was baptizing those who came to him. Why?

Matthew tells us that Isaiah was effectively speaking about John in Isaiah 40:3. What or who is Isaiah 40:3–5 a picture of? What, then, is John the Baptist's role?

In 1:1—4:16, Matthew quotes frequently from the Old Testament. What is his purpose in doing so? Why does he particularly do so in these early chapters?

Many people came to John. Speculate a little as to their various motives. Generally, what was their response?

Pharisees and Sadducees: a warning of things to come (Matthew 3:7–9)

 Read Matthew 5:20; 9:11; 9:14; 12:2; 15:1–2; 23:13–15. Who, for Matthew, were the Pharisees and Sadducees? What were their particular traditions and beliefs?

John attacks them fiercely. But they haven't done anything yet! Why does Matthew record this at this point?

What is the failing that John the Baptist accuses them of? What does Matthew think of their attitude to God?

Where has Matthew mentioned Abraham already in his Gospel?

What was the link he made there?

What does Matthew mean to convey to the reader by referring to Abraham? What point is Matthew making about the Pharisees and Sadducees and Jesus?

The Pharisees and Sadducees later become Jesus' main opponents. In what ways might we fall into the trap they have fallen into? In what ways do we take our status as children of God for granted? Be specific!

Jesus (Matthew 3:10–15)

This is the first we hear of Jesus as an adult. What sort of picture does Matthew paint of him, and what word or words would sum him up, as Matthew describes him? Why does Matthew introduce Jesus in this way?

Compare verses 8 and 10: what contrast does John make? Examine verse 12: again, what contrast does John make? What do these contrasts signify? Why does John not allow for any middle ground?

According to Matthew, which side are the Pharisees and Sadducees on? Why?

Which side are we on? What makes the difference? What are the consequences, for good or for bad, of the choice people make here?

Jesus, God's beloved Son (Matthew 3:11–17)

Why does Jesus ask to be baptized? What does this tell us about him?

Contrast Jesus' motives with what we have heard of the Pharisees and Sadducees. What does this suggest about our motives and actions? Who are we most like? What can we do about it?

Why does the Holy Spirit descend upon Jesus at this point? What lies immediately ahead of Jesus (4:1; 4:17)?

Who is speaking in verse 17, and why is this significant? Why does Matthew save this for last?

What is Matthew telling us in verse 17 about the *person* and *work* of Jesus? Don't just repeat the words of the verse: use your own!

What do these insights mean for us, practically, today?

Brainstorm

In this section Matthew has introduced the key players in the story and has hinted at what may be areas of confrontation later on. He has also told us that Jesus is the Messiah, the son of David, the son of Abraham and God's Son. Glance through 1:2—4:16 and brainstorm what parts of this section of the Gospel underline each of these aspects.

A response

God has proclaimed Jesus to be his beloved Son. Jesus has come to bring in the kingdom of heaven. Spend some time together in worshipping him.

The Holy Spirit descended upon Jesus to prepare him and empower him for his ministry. John has promised that Jesus will baptize us with the Holy Spirit and with fire. Spend time together meditating on this. Ask Jesus for his Holy Spirit to be more active in your life.

 GROWTH POINTS

2 Ministry and authority

This time we look at the second section of Matthew's Gospel, which we have called 'The proclamation of Jesus'. The theme of this section is 'Repent, for the kingdom of heaven has come near.'

In this story, Jesus has dealings with the sick, the Jewish authorities, tax collectors, sinners, John's disciples, and crowds far and near. In exploring his relations with them, we can learn much about how, as Christians today, we should relate to the world around us. Read the passage and consider the following discussion points.

Healing, forgiveness and authority (Matthew 9:1–8)

When the man comes to Jesus, Jesus' first action was to tell him that his sins are forgiven. Only later did he heal him physically. Why did Jesus act in this way?

What might Jesus' approach tell us about his concerns in healing people? What did he understand healing to be? How might this affect the way we approach healing today?

Jesus told the man he was forgiven without any public act of repentance on his part. How does this fit in with your understanding of repentance and forgiveness?

What are the keys phrases in this passage? What is Matthew telling us about Jesus and his ministry?

What are the various reactions here to Jesus' ministry? Why do those around Jesus react in these ways to him and to what he is doing?

In 10:14, 17–18, 23 Jesus forewarns the disciples about reactions to their ministry. In today's society what kind of reactions to our ministry should we expect? Do we come across any of these responses in our Christian ministry? Share relevant examples. Why does this happen? Or why not!?

Calling all sinners! (Matthew 9:9–13)

What did a tax collector do? How was he viewed by the society of the time?

How does the call of Matthew to discipleship add to Jesus' dealings with the paralysed man? What is the link between these two stories and these two people? What does this tell us about calling and discipleship today?

What did it mean to eat with somebody in Jesus' society?

Jesus ate with these tax collectors and sinners. These were people on the very edge of the 'community of faith'. How were they different from 'the crowd' (verse 8)? How were they different from the teachers of the Law? Why does Jesus attack the teachers of the Law but consort with these sinners?

There is no indication that Jesus required these sinners to repent first (or to sign a statement of faith!). Who are our modern-day 'outsiders'? Be specific. How should we relate to those who may be on the edges of our 'community of faith'? Welcome often risks compromise or accommodation. How welcoming should we be? How much compromise should we risk? Use specific examples. In view of verses 12–13, what is Jesus' mission? What is ours?

New and old ways (Matthew 9:14–17)

Why did John's disciples fast? What were their motives?

Matthew 5:17 tells us that Jesus has come to fulfil the Law and the Prophets (i.e. the Old Testament), not to set them aside. Yet these verses suggest that the new ways of Jesus don't sit very easily with the old ways of Jewish tradition. Summarize in your own words what these two passages are saying, and how they may fit together.

Which of our ways of doing things fall into the category of fasting/old garments/old wineskins? Be specific. What do Jesus' words suggest about these things? How open to change does God want us to be? What about those of us who find change threatening?

Jesus' ministry and ours (Matthew 9:35–38)

In what ways were the people of Jesus' society 'harassed and helpless, like sheep without a shepherd'? Why did Jesus feel compassion for them?

To what extent are Jesus' insights about *his* society valid for *our* society? Spend some time analysing our society in terms of Jesus' words. (Lack of community? Loneliness? Pressure? Be specific!) What is our reaction to what we have discovered? How should we respond to what we see?

Verse 35 sums up what Jesus' ministry consisted of. How did his teaching, preaching and healing activities relate together? What, together, did they amount to?

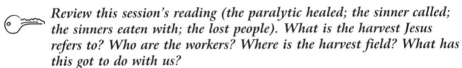

Review this session's reading (the paralytic healed; the sinner called; the sinners eaten with; the lost people). What is the harvest Jesus refers to? Who are the workers? Where is the harvest field? What has this got to do with us?

Summarizing the story

This section of Matthew's Gospel falls quite neatly into two sub-sections, 4:18—11:1 and 11:2—16:20. Our study today has been part of the first sub-section. The theme of this sub-section is the preaching, teaching and healing ministry of Jesus.

Scan through this sub-section (4:18—11:1). Summarize the story: what do Jesus and the disciples do? It may help you to use these passages as reference points: 4:18–22; 5:1—7:29; 8:1—9:34; and 10:1–42.

What have you learnt this time about the nature of Jesus' ministry?

A response

Spend time together remembering the needy people you have met in this study: the harassed and helpless; the sinners; the sick; the crowd. Recollect Jesus' compassion for them.

Focus on those in our society who fall into these sorts of categories. Ask God to give you more of Jesus' compassion for them. Offer yourself as a worker for the harvest field.

GROWTH POINTS

Matthew 11:1–6; 12:22–37

Some responses to Jesus

In the last session we looked at the preaching, teaching and healing ministry of Jesus in Galilee. This session looks at reactions to Jesus' ministry. We again meet various groups of people—John the Baptist and his disciples, the crowds and the Pharisees. We see their various responses to Jesus. We hear his answers to them. Through these interactions we explore who Jesus is and what he means for us and for our world.

'Are you the Coming One—or should we expect another?' (Matthew 11:1–6)

How would you describe John the Baptist and his disciples? Where do they stand in relation to Jesus? What is on their minds?

One writer (E. Appleton, *Church Times*, 30 April 1993) asserts provocatively: '... almost everyone wrestles with major questions about faith, unless they are brain-dead or bullied into concealment, even from their own selves...' Our doubts and questions often centre not so much on who Jesus is, but more on God's involvement in a troubled and dangerous world. Do we, as Christians, ever have doubts or uncertainties? What kind of doubts are they? What are they about? How deep do they go? What situations give rise to such doubts? Give specific examples.

Is such questioning permissible? How free do we feel to share doubts with others? What restrictions do we experience here? From inside ourselves? From outside?

How free should we feel to share such thoughts? Where and how could we share them? With whom might you feel able to share and discuss any doubts you have?

Psalms (such as 74, 79 and 88) sometimes express doubts and questions. How were the Psalms used and how are they used now? To whom do the Psalms express such thoughts? What might the Psalms suggest as appropriate contexts within which to explore and express our doubts?

Verse 6 offers boundaries of a kind to our questionings. What kind of boundaries are these and how do we keep to them? How might we help those who, through depression or deep experience of doubt, find such boundaries difficult to keep to?

Jesus doesn't answer John's question directly. Why not? He points his questioners to his words of *proclamation* and acts of *healing*. But how are they to use this information to arrive at an answer? What is required of them?

We must answer John's question too, for ourselves. But we cannot experience Jesus' earthly ministry in exactly the way John did. On what, then, might we today base our answer? What words? What actions? What evidence?

'Could this be the Son of David?' (Matthew 12:22–23)

Referring back to 9:35–38, describe 'all the crowds'. Where do they stand in relation to Jesus?

Who are the nearest equivalents of 'all the crowds' in our situation? Describe them. Why do they often waver or fall away? What can we do to help them come to faith?

'It is only by Beelzebub...' (Matthew 12:24–29)

We have met the Pharisees before. In 3:7 John called them a brood of vipers. In 9:3, they were beginning to turn against Jesus. Where do they stand in relation to Jesus now?

Their stance is illogical: verses 26 and 27. Why do they respond as they do? What motivates them—religion, power, security? What kind(s) of people today might act in similar ways?

In what ways does Jesus picture the in-coming of the kingdom of heaven in these verses? To what extent are these pictures valid for our ministry today? How might they affect how we carry out our ministry to the world and to those about us?

Look, for example, at Mark 4:30–34. What other ways are there of picturing the in-coming of the kingdom of God? How might those other pictures also affect how we carry out our ministry?

Opposing Forces (Matthew 12:30–37)

 In the context of Jesus' controversies with the Pharisees, what does 'blasphemy against the Spirit' (NRSV) or 'speaking against the Holy Spirit' (NIV) mean? What does it not mean!? How should Christians today approach this issue?

In the context of verses 33–37, what does Jesus mean in verse 36? Again, what does he not mean!? How should Christians today approach this issue?

 Many people we meet are uncertain about Jesus or unconvinced about him. Fewer are implacably opposed to him. We want to be open and welcoming to them, but we also want to be clear and firm on basic matters of faith. In the light of verse 30, how should we minister and witness to them? Use specific examples.

Summarizing the story

 This session and the previous two have focused on how Matthew prepares the way for Jesus' ministry, on how Jesus' ministry expresses itself in teaching, preaching and healing, and on people's reactions to his ministry. Spend a few minutes recalling, from these three sessions, who Matthew says Jesus is, what his ministry was like, and what the reactions to it were.

A response

If you have doubts about any aspect of your faith, or about how Christianity relates to the world we live in, acknowledge them together before God. Remember that he will honour the sincerity with which doubts are faced and wrestled with. Ask him to help you work through them. Ask him for the faith to stick with him as you do so.

Each of you offer to the group for prayer one person you know who is uncertain or unconvinced as to who Jesus is, or even simply hostile to him at the moment. You may wish to pray together for these people.

GROWTH POINTS

4 Matthew 16:21—17:9
Passion and transfiguration

With our fourth session we embark upon the third section of Matthew's Gospel, which we have entitled 'The passion and resurrection of Jesus'. The remaining studies explore this theme.

This time we look at Jesus' predictions of his death and resurrection, at the disciples' responses, and at the teaching Jesus gives; and we also explore Jesus' transfiguration.

Passion predicted (Matthew 16:21)

Jesus says he must go to Jerusalem. Track his journey there (the following verses may help: 17:22; 17:24; 19:1; 20:29; 21:1; 21:10). Why Jerusalem? What for? Why 'must'?

This verse is one of three passion predictions in this section of the Gospel. Look up 17:22–23 and 20:17–19, and compare and contrast them with this passage. How do these verses differ? What is the total picture they give? What are the disciples' responses in each case?

Jesus contradicted (Matthew 16:22–23)

Compare Peter's response with his confession in 16:16. In what way(s) is his confession there shown to be inadequate? What does he believe Jesus' role as Messiah involves?

How reasonable or unreasonable is Peter's response? How would you have reacted?

Why was Jesus' reply to Peter so fierce?

Why isn't Peter right? If God is God, all-powerful and all-knowing, why do you think the 'things of God' should involve betrayal, suffering, death, and only then raising to life?

Life through death (Matthew 16:24–28)

What does 'wanting to save our life' (verse 25) mean? In what specific ways do we—both as individuals and as a church—'want to save our life' today? Be as specific as you can—give examples in the areas of job, home life, Christian ministry and so on.

What does 'losing our life' (verse 25) mean? In what specific ways are we—as individuals and as a church—called to 'lose our life' today? Be as specific as you can and give examples.

We are called to deny ourselves, take up our cross and follow Jesus (16:24). What will this mean for us, in our present circumstances?

'This is my Son...' (Matthew 17:1–9)

Look up 4:8; 5:1; 15:29 and 28:16. At other significant points in his ministry Jesus ascends a mountain. What might this signify here?

What does the presence of Moses and Elijah suggest? Why are they there?

What does this event communicate to us about Jesus? What is your response to the picture it draws of him?

Only Matthew records that '...his face shone like the sun...' (verse 2). Why does he report this? Who is it meant to remind us of (see Exodus 34:29)? Why?

The transfiguration is reported *here* for a reason. Verse 5 in particular echoes what was said at Jesus' baptism (3:17). How does it add to what was said there?

In 16:16, 21, 22–23, 24–26 we read about who Jesus is, what he had to do, how Peter reacted, and what it means to follow Jesus. These verses are almost immediately followed by the transfiguration. What does it, and 17:5 in particular, add to those verses?

Jesus has been talking about his forthcoming death and resurrection. He has told his disciples that they are called to emulate him. Now they are told to 'listen to him'. What does this passage tell us about Jesus' authority and about how we should respond to him today? How might we set about 'listening' to him nowadays?

Peter wants to make this mountain-top experience *last* (verse 4). Why? To what extent do we prefer to keep to the 'spiritual heights' and avoid the 'spiritual depths'? Again, why? What does today's study passage (and especially 16:24) say about this?

A response

Review what you have discovered this session about who Jesus is and what he came to do. Respond to these insights by worshipping him, perhaps in song, or in prayer, or in silence.

In what specific ways have you been challenged as a disciple of Jesus this session? Offer this to God (in prayer, or in silence, or whatever) and ask him to enable you to follow Jesus better.

GROWTH POINTS

5 A question of authority

This session we follow Jesus into Jerusalem, the heart of the religious establishment and the place where he must suffer and die. In Jerusalem we look further into the developing confrontation between Jesus and the Jewish authorities. They ask him a question, and Jesus responds with a counter-question, two parables and an assertion.

'By what authority...?' (Matthew 21:23–27)

 Authority can come from different sources and be used in different ways. What kind of authority might the chief priests and elders of the people have in mind here?

What, do you think, is their *motivation* in confronting Jesus like this?

How do we react when our expectations or our power base are threatened? What particular things in the life of our church have threatened us, or threaten us at the moment, in this way? Be specific! Why do we react like this? How could we react differently? What would help us to do so?

Is the Jewish authorities' approach to be found in the Church today? Where? How could this sort of approach be avoided?

Why does Jesus link the question of John's authority to the question of his own? Is it just a clever debating trick, or is there more to it than that?

'What do you think...?' (Matthew 21:28–32)

 Why does Jesus tell them a parable here? Why not just start with 'I tell you the truth...' (verse 32)? What does the parable do?

Think about the parable together. Who, in Jesus' society, is the first son meant to represent, and why? Who, in Jesus' society, is the second son meant to represent, and why?

 What about today? Who is like the first son? Relate this question for your own life and journey of faith.

What people, today, are like the second son? Who are they? Where are they to be found?

'Listen to another parable...' (Matthew 21:33–41)

Why does Jesus tell another parable? How does it add to the first one?

Who, in Jesus' context, do the various characters in the parable represent?

Explore this parable together. Why not do a role-play based on it? To do this, one or more members (depending on your numbers) should take the role of the landowner, the tenants, the slaves, the son, and the 'other tenants'. Act the parable out, either dramatically, or talk it through as you sit together. As best you can, try to allow yourself to 'be' the person whose role you have taken. Afterwards, discuss how it felt to be the landowner, son, etc. What went on? What new insights—into the parable, into yourselves, into the Church and into society—did you gain? Don't forget to return to 'normality' afterwards!

'Therefore I tell you...' (Matthew 21:42–46)

How are verses 42 and 43 related? What are the characteristics of those who have the kingdom taken away from them? What are the characteristics of those who are given it?

What does Jesus mean by a people who produce the fruits of the kingdom?

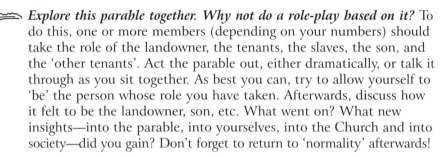

In what specific ways am I producing the fruits of the kingdom? In what ways am I not? What steps could I take here?

In what specific ways is our church producing the fruits of the kingdom? In what ways is it not? What steps could it take here?

In what specific ways is the wider Church producing the fruits of the kingdom? In what ways is it not? What steps could it take here?

A response

Much of this study has been about human *power* and divine *authority*. What have I learnt about myself this session? What areas of my life do I like to keep control over? Offer these areas to God.

In what areas could I—with God's help—produce more fruits of the kingdom? Ask God for the help of his Holy Spirit.

GROWTH POINTS

Matthew 26:57–68; 27:1–2, 11–31

Religious and political trial

This time we move steadily closer towards Jesus' suffering and death as we study Matthew's account of Jesus' trial before the Jewish authorities and before Pontius Pilate. The first and second parts of the session ask us to use our minds. The third part takes us on to the crucifixion, asks us to use our imagination, and brings us to worship.

'Tell us if you are the Messiah, the Son of God' (Matthew 26:57–68)

What have Jesus' dealings with the authorities been like during the course of our studies? Why should they want to put him to death? In what way does 27:18 clarify your understanding of their motives?

Why does Jesus 'remain silent' in the face of their evidence? Read Isaiah 53:7 and Psalm 38:12–22. Seen through the lens of Matthew's story, what do these passages tell us about Jesus' person and ministry?

Explore Jesus' very first words under oath: 'You have said so' (NRSV). What is the tone of Jesus' reply, and why does he respond like this? What truth, and what falsity, is to be found in the high priest's question?

'Are you the king of the Jews?' (Matthew 27:1–2; 11–26)

What are the motives behind Pilate's opening question?

What is the tone of Jesus' reply, and why does he respond as he does? What truth, and what falsity, is to be found in Pilate's question?

Why, apart from this, does Jesus remain silent?

Review the three passion predictions of 16:16, 17:22–23 and 20:17–19. How do they tie in with this passage? What does this tell us about God's intentions and the intentions of Jesus' opponents?

What might Matthew mean to convey by recording the crowd's desire to crucify Jesus and particularly by reporting their words at verse 25? How acceptable is this sentiment today?

Read Romans 11:1–6, 11–27. How does Paul explain the role of the Jewish nation in God's salvation? How might the Romans passage act as a corrective and an expansion of Matthew's views in 27:25?

How might we approach 27:25 as twentieth-century Christians who live in the shadow of the Holocaust and who bear part of the responsibility for its horrors?

Persecution and crucifixion (Matthew 27:27–54)

 John Calvin suggested that this spectacle of Jesus' love under fierce persecution should move us to 'secret meditation, not fancy words'. Taking our lead from him:

• Read the passage aloud, slowly, in four sections: verses 27–31, 32–37, 38–44, 45–54. Read right through to the crucifixion and the onlookers' reaction, stopping at verse 54.

• Spend time in silence together meditating upon the passage. Try to enter into the details of the scene in your imagination. Look quietly onto the scene, and allow it to speak to you. Or try to enter into what Jesus was feeling. Or into the minds of the soldiers and bystanders. Take your time over this. Take as long as you need.

• Spend some time quietly and reflectively sharing together what you have discovered about Jesus and about yourselves.

• Use this as a springboard for worship—quiet song, prayer of adoration, more silence. This worship is to be your response to what you have discovered in this study.

 GROWTH POINTS

7 The great commission

With this study we reach our final reading in the third section of Matthew's Gospel. It is a fitting place to end: for this passage sends Jesus' followers—then and now—out on a mission.

The reading for this session is the whole of chapter 28; but we concentrate on verses 16–20. Those verses may help us to think about our mission as...

- individuals
- a home group
- a church

in...
- our work-places
- our homes
- our neighbourhood.

Meeting the risen Jesus

Verse 17 mentions both worship and doubt. What do you think Matthew means here? Who is doubting? How do worship and doubt fit together here?

In session 3 we looked at the subject of doubt. In what ways might this passage take that discussion further?

Authority

Much of this study course has been about Jesus' authority. Summarize together what you have discovered already about Jesus' authority from Matthew's Gospel.

How does this passage add to this? What do we learn here about Jesus' authority? Try to put this in your own words.

What does this mean for us as Christians in our community today? Where, specifically, has Jesus' authority been particularly evident for you lately? Where less so? In what specific areas might the fact of Jesus' universal authority encourage you in your ministry?

Mission

What are the elements of Jesus' commission in verses 19 and 20? What aspects of mission is Jesus (and Matthew) concentrating on here?

Which aspects of Jesus' commission do you find hardest? What could be done to encourage you further here?

What, specifically, might Jesus' commission to make *disciples* and teach *obedience* to his commands mean today...

• for your home group

• for your church

• for you in the communities where you live and work?

In what specific ways might improvements be made? How might you set about doing things better? (Be positive; don't be too hard on yourselves!)

Presence

The disciples are promised that Jesus is with them. What is the context of that assurance?

Christians are sometimes told by others that they use their faith as a crutch. How might the context of this assurance suggest differently?

In what particular ways have you known the truth of this assurance lately in your day-by-day witness to Jesus? In what ways have you felt it to be lacking? Why? What might you do about this?

A response

Thank God together for the new insights you have gained this session.

Pray together about any problems or issues which have surfaced.

Read meditatively verses 18–20. Reflect on them quietly together.

GROWTH POINTS

Introduction: Studying Matthew: why and how?

There are at least *two* basic aims in these studies in Matthew's Gospel. The first is to study seven specific passages in the Gospel; the second is to gain a more general understanding, or overview, of what the Gospel is about.

These aims are interwoven. Matthew's Gospel isn't a thrown-together collection of stories or bits of teaching. It has been assembled with care and skill, and for particular reasons. One commentator notes that 'it reveals not only a meticulous concern... in the arrangement of its details, but also an architectonic grandeur in its totality'! So we can't just treat it piecemeal. The better we understand the whole Gospel, its purpose, and why it was written the way it was, the better we shall understand the specific texts we turn to. And the more we study specific texts, the better we shall understand the Gospel as a whole.

So it's worth thinking about Matthew's Gospel in overview before we look at individual passages. How then shall we analyse it? Where you start on such a venture will affect where you end up! Over the years scholars have had a go at looking at Matthew in various ways. The aim here is to give you an insight to a little of this thinking, in as accessible a way as possible. There are two approaches relevant to our purposes.

The 'teaching' approach

Some scholars see Matthew as made up of five 'books', preceded by a prologue (chapters 1–2) and followed by an epilogue (chapters 26–28).

Each 'book' contains a chunk of story and a 'discourse', or chunk of teaching. (These 'discourses' are the Sermon on the Mount, chapters 5–7; the 'missionary discourse', chapter 10; the 'parables of the kingdom', chapter 13; the discourse of chapter 18; and the 'eschatological discourse' of chapters 24–25). Parallels are sometimes drawn between these 'books' and the Old Testament books of Genesis to Deuteronomy, known as the Pentateuch.

This way, the *teaching* and *rule-making* elements of Matthew are emphasized and the *story* element minimized. The Gospel becomes essentially a teaching Gospel.

But there are problems with this approach.

• To call chapters 26–28 an 'epilogue' makes them an afterthought; in fact, they are arguably a climax to the Gospel.

• The books of the Pentateuch don't really seem to have many links at all with Matthew's 'books'.

• Exponents of this approach find difficulty in explaining how, in each 'book', the 'discourses' fit together with the story that surrounds them. There is much disagreement as to whether each chunk of 'discourse' is to be linked to the story before or after it.

• There is much 'discourse' within the story sections, and vice versa. This means that it may be wrong to draw too strong a contrast between 'discourse' and story sections in Matthew.

• Matthew's picture of Jesus isn't primarily one of teacher, as this approach implies. The disciples call him Lord more often than teacher or rabbi. Matthew is probably more concerned to convey that Jesus is Son of God than that he is a teacher.

The 'story' approach

A second possible approach is that the Gospel can be broken down into three basic sections, based upon the introductory statement of 1:1 ('The book of the origin of Jesus Christ...') and the formula statements in 4:17 and 16:21: 'From that time Jesus began...'. In this way, we can suggest the following structure:

1:1—4:16	*The preparation for Jesus*
4:17—16:20	*The proclamation of Jesus*
16:21—28:20	*The passion and resurrection of Jesus*

This analysis tends to stress Jesus as Son of God and Messiah, and minimizes his role as teacher. This is because the structure adopted concentrates upon storyline rather than teaching. This approach seems to fit the material better. For example, the first section, 1:1—4:16, demonstrates that Jesus is son of Abraham, son of David, and God's Son. The second section closes (16:16) with Peter's confession of Jesus as Son of God. The third section climaxes with the death of Jesus, which also demonstrates his divine Sonship, and ends with Jesus' command to baptize in the name of the Son.

According to Bauer (page 73), this structure can be developed further:

• within each of these sections, verses 1:1, 4:17 and 16:21 are general *headings* which are expanded in the material found later in that section;

• each of these sections builds up towards its respective *climax*;

• the first section (1:1—4:16) establishes the background for the rest of the Gospel (4:17—28:20), while the second section (4:17—16:20) provides the basis for the third (16:21—28:20). By this means, there is a sense of movement or *progression* throughout the whole Gospel.

There are some problems with this approach too:

• It may not account fully for the large blocks of 'discourse' or teaching obviously present in the Gospel. However, the repeated themes discerned by this approach are found both in the 'discourse' material as well as in the story material.

• This approach has not yet been adopted by most scholars.

But, that apart, it seems to fit the material quite well. We will be using some of these insights from the 'story' approach in the studies which follow.

We take the first study, on chapter 3, from the first section, 1:1—4:16; studies two and three from the second section, 4:17—16:20; and the rest from the third section, 16:21—28:20.

Details of the first section (1:1—4:16), our first study (chapter 3), and its individual verses are given in the leader's notes that follow.

1 Matthew 3:1–17
Preparation for ministry

Aims

• To appreciate 1:1—4:16 as a 'curtain-raiser' to Matthew's Gospel.

• To explore chapter 3 as the climax to the first section of Matthew's Gospel.

• To look at what Matthew has to say about the roles of John the Baptist, the Pharisees and Sadducees, and about the person and work of Jesus.

• To relate those insights to our actions and motives today.

• To enhance our *understanding* and *worship* of Jesus as Son of God.

NB There are *three* double pages for this week's study notes.

Introduction to the first section of the Gospel (Matthew 1:1—4:6)

Our first study comes from this first section of Matthew's Gospel. There are several points to note about this section.

It is probable that 1:1 is a *heading*. Not so much a heading for the whole Gospel. More a heading for this first section, 1:1—4:16. A major reason for this: the themes of

Jesus as 'Christ', 'son of David' and 'son of Abraham' are included in 1:1, are of special concern within the genealogy which follows, and are expanded upon in the first section, 1:1—4:16.

This section is bound together by three distinctive themes. First is the theme of *preparation for Jesus' ministry*. Note the following:

• All the events of this section take place before Jesus' public ministry starts. The first reference to that ministry is in 4:17.

• With the exception of Jesus, none of the major characters of the rest of the Gospel appear in this section. The disciples appear first in 4:18. The crowds in 4:23. Jesus' eventual opponents are mentioned, it is true, in 3:7. But they are not yet pictured as opposing Jesus.

• In this section Jesus does none of the things he does later: no preaching, healing, teaching, casting out of demons. He says nothing about his passion.

These points, together with the role of John the Baptist as Jesus' herald, show that this section is a preparatory one—a curtain-raiser, a sneak preview.

The second theme is this: in this section there are a number of quotations from the Old Testament. Matthew is particularly concerned in this section to demonstrate that Jesus is the *fulfilment of Old Testament expectations*. We will find several quotations in chapter 3.

The third theme: in this section there is a recurring stress on the *person* of Jesus. The picture of Jesus which Matthew gives us in this first section is meant to influence how we read the story of Jesus' ministry and passion. Bauer (page 78) puts this neatly: 'In 1:1—4:16 Matthew presents the person of Jesus *directly* to the reader; in 4:17—16:20 Jesus is revealed primarily in terms of his *public pronouncements*; and in 16:21—28:20 he is presented primarily in terms of his *passion*' (my emphasis).

In our passage from the first section, the person of Jesus is witnessed to by John the Baptist and by God himself. What God says about Jesus stands as the climax to this first section. The witness to Jesus comes from God himself. Jesus is announced as much more than son of David or of Abraham—but as the very Son of God.

What are the implications of all this?

• This first section of the Gospel, 1:1—4:16, is designed to prepare the reader for the rest of the Gospel by presenting directly the nature and identity of Jesus. In other words, who Jesus is. We are given a kind of sneak preview of the rest of the story. This first section tells us how to read the rest of the Gospel. Here we are told that Jesus is son of David, and son of Abraham. But, above all, Son of God. Our first study especially stresses this.

• The function of this first section (and of the rest of the Gospel) is also to stress that Jesus' coming is the major turning point in salvation history. That is why Matthew presents Jesus as the fulfilment of Old Testament expectations.

These two themes—who Jesus is, and what Jesus has come to do—will come up in our first study and later on in the course.

So this first section, Matthew 1:1—4:16, is the *curtain-raiser* to the rest of the Gospel. None of the major players are yet really on the scene. Jesus' public ministry hasn't yet started. Because of this, we can't expect the story proper to get fully going in this first study. Matthew is setting the scene here. He wants to tells us who Jesus is, which will involve us in more ideas and less story in this first study than in later studies.

The group study passage (Matthew 3:1-17)

The 'story approach' to Matthew suggests that this chapter is the climax of the first section, 1:1—4:16. In this first section we find a sort of procession of witnesses: an angel, Herod (despite himself!), the Magi; then, in chapter 3, John the Baptist; and, finally, the star witness, God himself!

And not only does the quality of the *witnesses* improve. So also does the quality of the *evidence*. Matthew has hinted already that Jesus is God's Son. In 1:16, he has broken the flow of the genealogy ('X the father of Y') when he gets to Jesus ('Mary, of whom was born Jesus...'). This hints at something special about Jesus' conception. In 1:18–20 Matthew tells us Jesus was conceived by the Holy Spirit; but we're not yet told what this means. Then we have reference to a 'son' in the prophecy of 1:23. In 2:7–23, Jesus is repeatedly referred to as 'the child'. Again, this hints that Jesus is not Joseph's biological son.

All these indications lead up to the direct statement of 3:17: 'This is my Son...'! God himself vouches for Jesus. Later on, Peter will say the same (16:16), as will the Roman guards (27:54). God also makes the point again at the transfiguration (17:5).

But that's not all we have in this chapter. We also have the Pharisees and Sadducees. Matthew is taking us aside and giving us advance notice as to who they are, what they will do, and what the long-term consequences will be for them. John the Baptist's words (3:7) seem to us to come out of the blue and to be very harsh. But they are said because of the later actions of these people.

And then we have Jesus himself. In contrast to the Pharisees and Sadducees, who are arrogant (3:9), Jesus is humble, submitting himself to baptism (3:14–15). Yet Jesus has authority to judge (3:10,12), authority to baptize with the Holy Spirit and with fire (3:11), and God's power for ministry (3:16).

Verse-by-verse

Study notes and leader's notes quote from NIV unless stated otherwise.

1 John is introduced like an Old Testament prophet. 'In those days' sounds like the Old Testament: see Judges 18:1 and Daniel 10:2. It doesn't indicate a particular time-frame. It means 'The time came when...'. 'Desert' sounds Old Testament-like as well.

2 John is pictured as a herald. He sets the scene. He announces the approach of the kingdom of heaven. He doesn't say why or how. His message is, at first, stark and uncompromising. It is exactly the same as Jesus' in 4:17.

'Repent': signifies a turning away from evil and a returning to God.

'Kingdom of heaven' = 'kingdom of God' in Luke. It doesn't mean a place, but God's reign or rule.

'is near' = literally 'has approached'. There is a note of urgency. God's rule is about to come in.

3 A quotation from Isaiah 40:3. For Matthew, John is the fulfilment of that prophecy.

4 Describing John's clothes is an allusion to Elijah: 2 Kings 1:8. The return of Elijah was meant to precede the coming of the Messiah: Malachi 4:5. Matthew later identifies John as Elijah in 17:10–13.

5–6 'went out' means 'were going out to him'. Same with 'were [being] baptized'. This baptism is a sign of repentance. It is different from Christian baptism, which is initiation into the Body of Christ.

7 Matthew's wording agrees, with minor changes, with Luke 3:7–9. But with one difference. In Luke, John's words are directed against the Jewish crowds. In Matthew, they are directed against two sects within Judaism, who, for Matthew, represent unbelief and opposition to Jesus.

'Brood of vipers' is a vitriolic accusation, equalled only by Jesus himself: 12:34; 23:33. In Old Testament, snakes lead people astray and symbolize evil: Genesis 3:1, Psalm 58:4. The Pharisees were highly regarded by Jews of the time. They supplemented the written Law with an oral code, not out of legalism, but in an attempt to fulfil the Law better. The Sadducees didn't accept these oral additions.

9 The double reference to Abraham is telling. Matthew has made it clear in 1:1 that Jesus is the true descendant of Abraham. In contrast with the Pharisees and Sadducees, he is humble, submitting to baptism when he needn't. And it is ironic that they, who claim to know God because they are related to Abraham, should go on to reject Abraham's true son.

10 A powerful picture of impending judgment, pulling together verse 2 (the kingdom of heaven approaches: repent) and verse 8 (bear fruit in keeping with repentance).

11 John's baptism prepares for Jesus. Jesus' baptizing will be the real thing!

13 John *came* (verse 1) to herald Jesus. Now Jesus *comes*. After John's build-up, you expect someone or something majestic. Yet Jesus comes... to be baptized by him!

15 'To fulfil all righteousness': it may mean 'to fulfil the will of God'. It may mean 'to fulfil the Old Testament Law'. If righteousness signifies—as Old Testament usage suggests—the saving activity of God, it may mean 'to fulfil God's salvation'. Most commentators go for the first option.

16 Jesus' baptism is private, between Jesus and God: first, the Pharisees and Sadducees fall out of the picture after

verse 10; secondly, Matthew makes it clear that Jesus alone sees the Spirit of God. What does this signify? First, Jesus' baptism is not an act of proclamation. Second, this implies that we, the readers, are being given a sneak preview or advance notice of *who Jesus is* and *whose authority he has*.

God's words amount to a reference to Isaiah 42:1. But 'servant/child' there has been changed to 'son' here, probably under the influence of Ps 2:7. So Jesus is God's anointed one (Ps 2:7) and his chosen servant (Is 42:1).

'beloved': this is either an adjective ('my beloved Son' or 'my Son, whom I love'), or a title ('my Son, the Beloved'). If the latter, it may echo the title 'my chosen one' found in Isaiah 42:1.

To be precise, 'like a dove' doesn't refer to the appearance of the Spirit, but to the way it descended upon Jesus. It is in Luke 3:22 that we are told that the Spirit was in bodily form like a dove.

2 Ministry and authority

Aims

• To explore the nature and import of Jesus' public ministry.

• To consider Matthew's claim that Jesus has God's authority for his ministry.

• To explore how and why Jesus relates to those in need in his society, and how and why we should relate to those in need in our society.

• To allow the good news of the kingdom of heaven to challenge our complacency.

• To see how and why ministry gives rise to a range of responses, including opposition.

• To offer ourselves as workers in God's harvest.

Introduction to the second section of the Gospel (Matthew 4:17—16:20)

We are looking at the Gospel of Matthew as a story about Jesus. According to this approach, our second and the third studies form part of the second section of Matthew's Gospel. The first section had an introductory verse. So do the second and third sections (4:17;

16:21). In the case of sections two and three, these verses start with the same words: 'From that time on Jesus began to...'. They amount to a kind of chapter heading for the section which they open. The introductory verse to the second section announces Jesus' preaching ministry ('From that time on Jesus began to preach/proclaim...') and the content of that proclamation ('Repent...'). That is the theme of the second section of this Gospel. The introductory verse of section three (16:21) announces Jesus' passion and resurrection; and that is the theme of that third section of the Gospel.

There are several things to note:

• These introductory verses are expanded upon in the section which they introduce. So we can expect 4:17 to be taken up in our two studies on this section. Matthew does this not by formulating doctrinal statements or theological propositions, but by way of a story.

• This second section of the Gospel builds up, like the other sections, to a climax. In this case, it is Peter's confession of Jesus as Messiah and Son of the living God (16:16).

• Just as each section builds up to a climax, so does the whole of the Gospel. So, part of the job of the second section of the Gospel is to provide a basis or foundation for the third section, which is the climax to the whole Gospel.

• There is a further aspect to note. Arguably, the second section itself falls into two chunks. In 4:17—11:1, the theme is that of Jesus going about Galilee teaching, preaching the gospel of the kingdom and healing. The second chunk, 11:2—16:20, concentrates more on the rejection by Israel of that message and ministry. We have one study from each section.

It is the first sub-division of the second section (i.e. 4:18—16:20) of the Gospel that we are concerned with in this study. In summary, this is the storyline (Bauer, page 87). Jesus calls his disciples (4:18–22). He ascends the mountain and proclaims the character of and requirements for participation in the kingdom (5:1—7:29). He travels round Galilee, performing ten mighty acts (8:1—9:34). He sends out his disciples on a mission modelled on his own (10:1–42). He warns them that they can expect a negative response. And this warning serves as a lead-in to the second sub-division, with its theme of rejection.

In sum, then, the theme of Jesus' proclamation of the kingdom and call to repentance (4:17) is developed in the second section of the Gospel like this: *proclamation* of the kingdom (4:18—11:1) leads to *rejection* by Israel as a whole, but *acceptance* by the disciples (11:2—16:20).

The group study passage (Matthew 9:1–17, 35–38)

We take up the story at 9:1, where Jesus performs healing miracles.

Chapters 8 and 9 record them. They come *after* the Sermon on the Mount, where Jesus sets out the nature of the kingdom of heaven and the terms of participation in it, and *before* the disciples' own healing mission. These healing miracles are all about Jesus' authority: authority over the Law (9:5–7, 14–17), over demons and sickness (8:1–17; 28–34), over would-be followers (8:18–22), over the creation (8:23–27), and over sin itself (9:1–8). The two passages chosen first tell of Jesus' acts, together with some of his teaching (9:1–17), and then summarize Jesus' ministry, the reasons for it, and the need for labourers (9:35–38).

The story of the healing of the paralysed man (9:1–8) is paralleled in Mark 2:1–12 and Luke 5:17–26. It refers back to the angel's prophecy to Joseph (1:21): 'he will save his people from their sins'. Matthew doesn't spend time on the difficulty of getting to Jesus, the opening of the roof and so on. He gets to the guts of the story: the question of Jesus' authority. Similarly, removal of attention from the faith of the friends stresses the hostility of the authorities and the comments of the crowd.

The story of the call of Matthew and Jesus eating with sinners (9:9–13) has a common theme: Jesus has shown he has authority to forgive sins. He then goes on to call a sinner to discipleship. And, to show how radical the effects of Jesus' ministry are, he goes on to share a meal with sinners. He has the authority to call sinners to his service and to call (invite) them to table with him.

The story of a conflict over fasting (9:14–17) has a theme in common with what precedes it— feasting/drinking/fasting. But the area of dispute has moved from 'why eat with these people?' to 'why eat at all when you are supposed to fast?' Note that the controversy is raised not by the Pharisees and Sadducees but by John's disciples. The conflict becomes the occasion for Jesus to tell some parables on the nature of the kingdom he ushers in. He brings a joy (feasting) and a newness (new cloth/wineskins) which the traditions of conventional Jewish piety (fasting) cannot contain.

Verse-by-verse

2   Why does Jesus forgive the man's sin? There are at least three possibilities:

• Specific sins committed by the man were responsible for his condition.

• The onlooking teachers of the Law will have believed that that was so.

• The man's problem was not sin, but guilt, i.e. the inability to appropriate God's forgiveness.

The relationship of sin and suffering is too big a topic to be discussed in depth here. But here are some pointers:

• The witness of the Gospels seems varied. In John 9:3, Jesus refutes the idea that the blindness of one specific individual was owing to his or his parents' sin. However, in John 5:14,

Jesus does tell a lame man he had healed to stop sinning in case something worse befalls him.

• It is probably not in Matthew's mind to enter into a detailed discussion as to the link between sin/sins and suffering. His focus is on the authority of Jesus. So, as far as this study is concerned, this question is really a side-issue.

• More positively, there is a link of sorts. But it is the reverse of what you might expect. The question 'does sin lead to sickness' moves from sin to sickness. Jesus moves in the other direction, from sickness to sin. Seeing the man's sickness, he wants to offer him healing which isn't limited to the physical, but which includes the whole person.

3 'blaspheming': in their view, Jesus was taking upon himself an authority—to forgive sins—which belonged only to God.

4 'Why do you think evil in your hearts?': this fits with Matthew's narrative approach. In section one (1:1—4:16), we have a hint of the conflict to come: the Pharisees and Sadducees are described as a 'brood of vipers' (3:7). In this first part of section two (4:17—11:1), the conflict is not yet in the open: as yet they haven't done anything against Jesus. So far, their opposition is purely on the level of their thoughts and motives. The response of the Pharisees in 9:34 foreshadows the theme of the second sub-division (11:2—16:20), that of rejection of Jesus.

5 Jesus' question is asked 'from the standpoint of his opponents: it does not imply that communicating the pardon of God to a man is less difficult or less serious than healing his body' (Hill, page 171).

6 This verse stresses Jesus' authority. 'Son of Man': why is this title used? It must mean more than 'a human being' here, for the point is precisely that human beings in general do not have authority to forgive sins. On the other hand, this is the only time the ideas of 'Son of Man' and healing are brought together in the synoptic Gospels. It may be that the use of this term heightens the mystery rather than relieves it: the teachers are not told *who Jesus is*; they are simply shown, by his actions, *whose authority he has*.

8 'filled with awe': literally, 'they were afraid'. Matthew uses the same word at the transfiguration (17:6) and the resurrection (28:5, 10). The crowds represent a position between that of the teachers (unbelief) and the disciples (faith).

9 Tax collectors were despised as collaborators with the Roman authorities. 'Follow me': an invitation to become a disciple.

10 NIV's 'in Matthew's house' is an interpretation. The text says 'in the house': Matthew's or Jesus' house? See Luke 5:29. To eat with someone was to identify yourself closely with them. To eat with sinners was ritually to defile yourself. NIV's quotation marks ('sinners') are questionable. True, the Pharisees saw them as sinners (whether they were or not) because they wouldn't keep the oral law; but, on the other hand, they were (like everyone else) sinners in a real sense.

12 Again we have a link between sin and sickness. This time Jesus makes the connection: sinners are as if sick. Only the sick need a doctor. There is irony here. According to Matthew, the biggest sinners are the Pharisees, but they don't recognize their need of Jesus.

13 A quotation from Hosea 6:6. The word for 'mercy' is emphatic. For Jesus, mercy is much more important than the proper implementation of ritual. 'Call' is deliberately ambiguous: it can mean

to *call* to discipleship and to *invite* to a feast.

15 By 'bridegroom' Jesus is referring to himself. This may also be a veiled reference to the Jewish tradition of the Messiah. Hosea 2:16–20, Isaiah 54:5f and particularly 62:4f may have a bearing here.

16 The word for 'patch' also means 'fulness' or fulfilment'. This wordplay gives a direct link with 5:17: Jesus has come to fulfil the Law and the Prophets. But not by patching them up! Although in one sense the Law and the Prophets are not set aside (5:17), the traditional Jewish piety expressed here by John's disciples is incompatible with the newness and joy of the kingdom of heaven.

35 This verse is repeated in various forms throughout this first sub-division of the second section of the Gospel. The other occasions are 4:23 and 11:1. This repetition serves to stitch the sub-division (4:17—11:1) together and provide it with a framework. This verse stresses the *public* nature of Jesus' ministry.

37 This and the following verse provide a connection between Jesus' ministry (8:19–36) and that of the disciples (10:1–42). Verse 35 has summarized Jesus' public ministry: teaching, preaching, healing. Verse 37 sets the scene for the disciples' public ministry in chapter 10, which reproduces and mirrors Jesus' ministry in all respects, except that they do not teach (10:1, 6–8).

3 Some responses to Jesus

Matthew 11:1–6; 12:22–37

Aims

• To explore the nature, role and legitimacy of Christian doubt and enquiry, and to allow members to express areas of doubt or uncertainty in their lives.

• To reflect on the relationship of faith to doubt and enquiry.

• To extrapolate, from the responses of those around Jesus, to the responses to Jesus of the people who live and work where we do.

• To reflect on our ministry and witness to them and to others.

Overview

In sessions 2 and 3, we explore the second section of the Gospel, 4:18—16:20. This section can itself be broken down into two sub-sections. Last time's study came from the first sub-section, 4:18—11:1. The study comes this time from the second sub-section, 11:1—16:20. The first sub-section concentrated especially on the proclamation of Jesus and on his authority. Here, in the second sub-section, the emphasis is more on the response to Jesus' proclamation and ministry.

The group study passage (Matthew 11:2–6)

We have already seen something of the response of John's disciples to Jesus' ministry in 9:14f. This passage tells us more. They are beginning to have doubts as to who Jesus really is.

But this passage does something more: it gives us more of a handle on the identity of Jesus, and on the nature and purpose of his ministry. Already in 9:35f Matthew has linked Jesus' teaching, preaching and healing. There Matthew sees Jesus' ministry as a rounded whole; the teaching, preaching and healing aspects are integrally related to each other.

The same is clear from Jesus' answer here. Jesus puts together healing and bringing good news to the poor. *Each is a manifestation of the presence of the kingdom of heaven.* Preaching and healing are different activities, but they each, in their own way, point to the same thing: the inauguration of the kingdom of heaven in Jesus. Is the spoken word more powerful a witness to the kingdom of heaven, or more central to God's purposes, than actions? Not for Matthew: he suggests that, though words and actions are different, they are all of a piece in bringing in the kingdom of heaven.

Note also that Jesus is not just promising something for the future. The kingdom was coming in right then, in Jesus himself. See Jesus' words in 4:17.

What sort of response does Jesus' answer—and his ministry—call for? Jesus gives no cut-and-dried solution to who he is. Response to Jesus is not simply a matter of theory or analysis ('what category does Jesus fit?'). Room is left for *personal* decision. We are to answer the question: 'what does Jesus' coming and ministry mean for me or for us?'

With the questioning of John's disciples, Matthew leads us into the issue which dominates this sub-section: how do people respond to the person and ministry of Jesus? In 11:7–15 Jesus reflects further on John the Baptist, but not on his response to Jesus; rather, on the response of the crowds to John's proclamation of Jesus. From the crowds, Jesus turns to the response of 'this generation' to his ministry (11:16–19), and then on to the response of the cities in which he has done most of his ministry (11:20–24). This leads, in turn, to stories dealing with the response of the Pharisees to Jesus ministry (chapter 12).

What we have here, then, is a *procession of witnesses* to Jesus' ministry: John's followers and their response; the crowds and their response; 'this generation' and its response; the cities and their response; the Pharisees and their response. In each case, the question, 'Are you the Coming One or should we expect someone else?' (11:3) and the answer, 'Blessed is the one who takes no offence at me'

(11:6) together provide a framework or litmus test for evaluating their response and for applying what we find to the world we find ourselves in.

The group study passage (Matthew 12:22–37)

Selectively, we have looked at the response of John and his disciples. Now we look at that of the Pharisees. So far in chapter 12, the Pharisees have challenged Jesus and the disciples for (allegedly) breaking the sabbath by garnering food (1–2). Jesus' answer refers to David's use of the consecrated bread in 1 Samuel 21, and to the act of the priest on the sabbath. Next, he breaks the sabbath by healing (9–14), and the Pharisees' response is to plot to kill him (14). Matthew counters this by reflecting on Isaiah 42, the first servant song. He gives us the 'God's-eye' view. Jesus is the servant, chosen by God, anointed by his Spirit (17–21). The Pharisees are shown, then, to be acting contrary to God's purposes.

So far, then, Jesus hints that he is the son of David (3–4); he says he is the son of man (8); Matthew calls him the servant of God (17–21).

These themes are picked up in our passage, 12:22–37. The people ask 'Could this be the Son of David?'. The Pharisees respond that Jesus is the servant of the devil, not of God. So we have two polarized views. Matthew: Jesus is son of David and servant of God.

Pharisees: Jesus is servant of Beelzebub. In Jesus' terms (30), people are either for or against him. There is no middle ground. The Pharisees are clearly against him. Ironically, the very religious leaders who accuse Jesus of being in league with Beelzebub are themselves agents of Satan.

Jesus' answer exposes the flaws in the Pharisees' argument (25–26) and throws the question back to them and their associates (27). He then recasts the issue more positively: if Jesus works by God's authority, then the kingdom of God has come (28). The rest of the passage puts things very clearly into two categories. Those categories are pitched against each other: the robber and the strong man (29); those for and against Jesus (30); sin against human beings or Jesus and sin against the Holy Spirit (31–32); good and bad fruit and actions (33–37). Matthew sees the inauguration of the kingdom of heaven in starkly polarized terms. This may shock us, who are used to twentieth-century Western liberality. It may surprise those of us who believe in inclusiveness and open-handedness. All the same, we must take Matthew's stance on board and work through it.

Verse-by-verse

11:1 Last time we mentioned 4:23, 9:35 and 11:1 as summary passages which hold the Gospel's second section together. This verse is one of them. It acts as a clear end to the first subsection, 4:18—11:1: it rounds off the instruction of the disciples. And it acts as a beginning to the second sub-section, 11:2—16:20: it reintroduces the theme of Jesus' public teaching, which, as we shall see, will provoke more and more antagonism.

3 'the Coming One': John is referring to the Messiah. (The phrase will have been familiar because of the use of Isaiah 59:20 in synagogue worship). Matthew clearly wants us to understand this phrase in this way: he specifically refers to Jesus as 'Christ' or 'Messiah' in verse 2.

We aren't told what has provoked John's qualms about Jesus. The weight of this passage lies elsewhere:

• on the question of response to Jesus— note that John's question has both the positive and the negative in it;

• not on John's psychological condition, but on Jesus' answer to him.

5 This verse resonates with the language of Isaiah 29:18f, 35:5–6 and 61:1f. The 'poor' are those of Matthew 5:3, and the phrase refers in Matthew to those who follow God and recognize their need of him.

6 This verse crystallizes the theme of this second sub-section, that of the response of Israel to Jesus' ministry and the presence of the kingdom in him.

12:23 'all the people': better, 'all the crowds'. Emphatic, and only found here.
'astonished': a strong word in the Greek: literally, 'were beside themselves'.
The form of the question in the Greek shows that they are minded to answer 'no'. But, in Matthew's hands, the question has a double focus. It tells us what the crowd was asking. It addresses us too, and asks us to say *who we think Jesus is.*
Son of David: a popular title of the

time for the Messiah. Note a link here with 11:3: John's question and that of the crowd amount to this: Is Jesus the Messiah?

24 Beelzebub: refers to the prince of demons. It may be derived from 2 Kings 1:2–6 (*baal zebub*), meaning the Lord of the Flies, the god of Ekron. Or it may be an intended corruption of *baal zebul*, meaning Lord of the Abode on High. Or it might mean Lord of the House, in which case a play on words in 25 and 29 is possible.

25 'kingdom', 'city' and 'house' are units of organized power. Internal strife makes the continued existence of any such organization impossible. Even on the level of logic, the Pharisees' argument is flawed.

27 Jesus then turns the argument back on his attackers. The Pharisees' associates (literally, 'your sons') also profess to cast out demons. In whose power do they do it? If by Satan, what are the Pharisees doing condoning their activity? If by God, why can't they allow that Jesus' ministry is done by God also?

28 'has come upon you': the kingdom is not just near or pressing in; it has *actually arrived* in Jesus, even if not in its fulness. The 'upon you' is barbed: it has a double focus. In the case of the Pharisees and others opposed to Jesus, this will result in judgment and condemnation (36–37). In the case of those who acknowledge Jesus as Messiah, the positive aspects of verses 18–21 apply.
Only here does Matthew use 'kingdom of *God*' instead of 'kingdom of *heaven*'. This may be to stress the starkness of the battle between God and Satan.

29 No ethical content is intended here. Satan is the strong man; Jesus is the stronger!

31 Care is needed here—many Christians get anxious about blasphemy against the Spirit, and are far too ready to apply it to themselves. Context is vital. The Pharisees attribute Jesus' authority and power to Satan. They are implacably set against him. *That—and only that—is what is meant by blasphemy against the Spirit.* Even attacking Jesus is forgivable; but attacking the power by which he works is not. Those who are intransigently set against the power and activity of God put themselves, by their own actions, outside the sphere of God's salvation. 'Those who worry about the unforgivable sin cannot be guilty of it!' (Hare, page 141).

33 The Pharisees' blasphemy is not accidental or spontaneous: it arises from who they are inside. Actions arise out of orientation of character.

36 Another cause of Christian twitchiness! 'Every careless word': at its most literal, this could be interpreted so as to put every person, Christian or otherwise, in doubt of salvation. Again, note the context. Jesus is talking about those who are, root and branch, set against him, those whose idle words stem from the settled attitude of their lives against him. *Matthew does not have faithful members of the Christian community in mind here.*

34 'You brood of vipers': this takes us back to John's prophetic words in 3:7 (session 1) which are being fulfilled. There, as here, the picture of good fruit is used.

4 Passion and transfiguration

Aims

• To look at the first passion prediction in the light of the rest of Matthew's Gospel

• To explore the nature of Jesus' ministry, and particularly the suffering he was called to.

• To relate that to Christian discipleship today.

• To look at the transfiguration and relate it to the rest of Matthew's Gospel, particularly 16:16–28 and 3:13–17.

• To explore what Matthew says here about Jesus' nature, ministry and authority.

• To explore Peter's response, and to offer members the opportunity to deepen and extend their discipleship.

Introduction to the third section of the Gospel (Matthew 16:21—28:20)

This session we move into the third and final section of Matthew's Gospel, according to our framework. We have called this section (following Bauer) 'The passion and resurrection of Jesus'. In the introductory leader's notes

80

we noted three claims made by Bauer:

• Matthew 16:21 is an introductory heading to this third section, expanded upon later in the section, just as 1:1 and 4:17 were introductory verses to the first and second sections of the Gospel.

• Each section builds up to its respective climax. The climax to this section is Jesus' suffering, death and resurrection, together with his missionary commission. The four sessions we have in this section allow us to build up to that climax.

• The third section of the Gospel is itself the climax to the whole Gospel, prepared for by the first two sections.

Matthew 16:21 summarizes the content of this third section. The rest of the section expands upon this material.

So far in the Gospel, Jesus' death and resurrection have only been hinted at: see 9:15; 10:4; 10:38; 12:14; 12:39–40. Here Jesus talks about it explicitly for the first time. In this sense, 16:21 introduces the themes of the rest of the section. At this point, Matthew's account shifts up a gear.

The section moves gradually from this introductory verse to its climax. How does Matthew achieve this?

One method Matthew uses to move the story on to the climax is a geographical one: the idea of the *journey to Jerusalem*. The phrase

'...must go to Jerusalem...' is already present within 16:21, and it is outworked as Jesus moves through Galilee (17:22), to Capernaum (17:24), to beyond the Jordan (19:1), to Jericho (20:29), towards Jerusalem, arriving at the outskirts in 21:1 and in Jerusalem proper in 21:10.

Another method is a literary one: the technique of *repetition*. This is found in 16:21, 17:22–23 and 20:17–19. This third summary is the most complete of the lot.

These two techniques, the geographical and the literary, are linked (as Bauer, page 97, points out) since each of the predictions includes a reference to the journey to Jerusalem.

Thirdly, the movement of the *narrative itself* contributes to this progression to a climax. Bauer (page 98): 'Although [after Peter's confession in 16:16] the disciples now know who Jesus is, they are not yet ready to "go and make disciples of all nations" (28:19). They must first learn the true purpose of the messianic mission: suffering, death and resurrection. This Jesus sets out to do in 16:21—28:20.'

The group study passage (Matthew 16:21—17:9)

Our passage for this session picks up some of these themes. We have the first of the repeated passion predictions in 16:21. Within it, the journey to Jerusalem is mentioned. And, thirdly, Peter's response shows how far—despite his confession of 16:16—the disciples have to go in discerning the true nature of Jesus' ministry. Jesus' reprimand of Peter seems harsh; but we must bear in mind several factors:

• Peter to some degree represents the response of the rest of the disciples. Just as he pioneers their realisation in 16:16 of who Jesus is, so he also represents their short-sightedness in 16:22. If they cannot understand the real nature of Jesus' ministry, then nobody will!

• As Matthew has shaped his story, we are at a turning-point in Jesus' ministry. The passion and resurrection are predicted for the first time. From this point, the story builds up momentum and snowballs towards these climactic events. Peter's contradiction at this fulcrum point must be scotched.

As if in contradiction to and qualification of Peter's response, the transfiguration is recorded next, taking place six days later. God's words at the transfiguration echo his words at Jesus' baptism (3:17). But *this repetition is more than just repetition*, for two different reasons:

• It takes place after Peter's confession of Jesus as Messiah and Son of the living God in 16:16; after Jesus' prediction of his death and resurrection in 16:21; and also after Peter's contradiction of Jesus in 16:22. So this repetition of God's words serves as a confirmation of Peter's insight in 16:16, confirmation of Jesus' prediction in 16:21, and at the same time as a contradiction of Peter's rebuke in 16:22.

• God's words at the transfiguration add a phrase to his words at the baptism: 'listen to him!' This addition stresses Jesus' authority, and in doing so again, in the context of 16:16, 21 and 22, serves to underline Peter's confession, to stress Jesus' words about his death and resurrection, and to contradict Peter's rebuke.

Verse-by-verse

16:21 'From that time...': this marks a new phase in the Gospel—our third section. '...began to show...': not 'teach' (or 'explain', as NIV). This is a foretelling, a prediction of what must take place. '...that he must go...': an indication that this was God's will. No reason for this being God's will is given. For that we have to wait until 20:28: 'a ransom for many'.

22 'God forbid it...' literally '(God be) gracious to you...'.

23 A harsh rejoinder, used against Satan himself in 4:10. See comments above for thoughts on this. Peter could at the one moment acknowledge Jesus as Messiah, and yet fail to see that messiahship involved suffering. The first-century Jewish hope of a political redemption, with the Messiah as national saviour was an idea difficult to shake off. Peter's stance was, in that sense, understandable.
  There is a possible ironic wordplay here. Peter is *Petros*, the rock. Here, though, he is a rock (see Leviticus 19:14) for Jesus to stumble over!

24 Jesus turns now from addressing Peter, to the disciples.

His words are a variation upon 10:37–39. To deny oneself means (Hare, page 195) 'to subordinate the appetites and desires to God's will for us as made known in Jesus'. Taking up one's cross refers primarily to being willing to suffer ridicule and hostility for following Jesus.

These are probably not conditions for discipleship, but rather teaching as to what a life of discipleship means. This verse is linked to 16:21—so it shows that self-denial, taking up the cross, and following Jesus involve the same rigours that Jesus himself was facing. The verse is also linked to 16:22—showing that this understanding of discipleship was as yet beyond the disciples.

25 'life/soul': the Greek word *psyche* (and the Hebrew equivalent) signify the whole of one's being, that which makes you who you are, and can include the notions of life here-and-now and eternal life. But, within that, it is possible for the word to have various shades of meaning, depending on the context. Those various slants are being played around with here. In verse 25 the nuance seems to be 'him- or herself, one's whole being'. Jesus was to lose himself entirely at God's behest on the cross. Verse 26, however, seems to use the word more in the sense of 'eternal life, life in the age to come'.

Note the strong paradox of verses 25 and 26. This turning upside-down of what seems the normal order of things is an aspect of the cross and resurrection itself. The idea of the shameful death of the Messiah and Son of God is, to ordinary ways of thought, an inversion of the natural order. See 1 Corinthians 1:18f.

27 The possibility of gaining or losing life arises because judgment is imminent.

'...according to what he has done...': This doesn't support any developed notion of salvation by works. First, Jesus—and Matthew—have no such developed distinction in mind. It was only with Luther that the arguments between salvation by works and salvation by grace became so polarized. The New Testament supports the position that faith is primary, but that it is evidenced by works. For Matthew's position see 3:10 and particularly 12:33–37.

28 What does 'the Son of Man coming in his kingdom' refer to for Matthew? Probably not the second coming. However imminent Jesus thought the second coming would be, by Matthew's time it had not come; and an interpretation involving the second coming does not sit well with what Matthew records in 24:14. Commentators suggest the transfiguration, the resurrection, the fall of Jerusalem in AD70, or the gift of the Holy Spirit. The reason the saying is here appears to be to bolster up the disciples as they consider the nature of discipleship.

17:1 A mountain is, amongst other things, the place where the nature of Jesus' identity and ministry is often revealed. See 4:8; 5:1; 15:29; 28:16. This revelation involves only the inner circle of Jesus' disciples, the Three.

The mountain is traditionally identified as Mount Tabor, or else Mount Hermon.

The exact time reference is unusual. It may be meant to bring to mind Exodus 24:16f, where the glory of the Lord settled on Mount Sinai.

2 'transfigured': literally 'changed'. Here the disciples have a glimpse of Jesus' end-time glory.

The presence of Moses and Elijah may indicate that the witness of the Law (Moses) and the Prophets (Elijah) supports Jesus as Messiah. Or perhaps the presence of Moses suggests a contrast between his face, which shone with derived glory when he met God (Exodus 34:29), whilst Jesus' face shines with an underived glory, appropriate to his identity as Son of God. Elijah, certainly, is seen as the forerunner of the Messiah: Mark 9:11; Matthew 17:10.

4   Peter is out of his depth! Does his desire to stay on the mountain-top suggest that he still remains happier with what we might call 'peak experiences', and that he remains unwilling to go back down the mountain, where (verse 9) Jesus will instruct them more about his suffering and resurrection? There certainly seems an attempt to make permanent a temporary moment of revelation.

5   See comments above for the force of this verse. In this account we have both revelation by vision and by word.

5 A question of authority

Matthew 21:23–46

Aims

• To explore the Jewish authorities' motives in their dealings with Jesus.

• To work from this into issues of power and authority today, and into our motives as individuals and as a church.

• To explore some of the depth of two of Jesus' parables.

• To allow the parables to speak to members about the range of responses to Jesus and their own responses to him.

• To reflect on how involvement in the kingdom of heaven is related to our response to Jesus himself.

Overview

This is the second of four studies in the third and final section of Matthew's Gospel, extending from 16:21—28:20, which we have entitled 'The passion and resurrection of Jesus'.

The last leader's notes pointed out that this section moves to a climax, and that Matthew achieves this by (amongst other things) a technique of geographical progression. We might call that progression 'The journey to Jerusalem'.

The events in today's passage occur once Jesus has entered Jerusalem. Jerusalem is the place of Jesus' trial, crucifixion and resurrection, and so a fitting place for the climax to occur. We will see that our passage foreshadows Jesus' death in the parable of the Vineyard.

Jerusalem is also the place where confrontation with the Jewish authorities comes to a head; and it is that process of increasingly vehement controversy which our passage concentrates on.

Chapters 21–23 deal with events in Jerusalem. But the picture is not a static one. Here too there is movement and progression.

First, *geographical progression.* Jesus is shown to mover closer and closer to the geographical heart of the religious establishment of his day. As he does so, opposition increases, and his death comes closer:

• In 21:1–11 he enters the city, on an ass.

• In 21:12 he enters the temple and overturns the tables. The temple is the prime symbol of the authority of the Jewish religious establishment over the religion of Israel and of its power over its adherents. Jesus' actions are, therefore, a threat to that authority and power. So it is likely that *the question of Jesus' authority* will arise. We have seen something of this before already: in

12:24f the authorities accused Jesus of working in league with Beelzebub. But here the issue of Jesus' authority becomes even more pressing, and gives rise to very harsh words of judgment from Jesus and a final break between him and the authorities.

Secondly, *dramatic progression.* Jesus enters Jerusalem. He overturns the temple tables. The children shout his praises. The authorities object and Jesus replies with Scripture. He leaves for Bethany near by. He enters the temple again. There controversy arises, without being resolved: 21:23–27. This controversy gives rise to three parables (21:28–32; 21:33–41; 22:1–14—often called the 'parables against Israel'), with an Old Testament quotation and some comment interposed between the second and third parables (21:42–46). In chapter 22 more controversy follows. This gives rise, in chapter 23, to Jesus' pronouncement of woes over the scribes and Pharisees. At the end of the chapter, as Jesus leaves the temple for the Mount of Olives to teach the disciples, he pronounces the temple desolate (23:38). From this point, the Jewish authorities are seen as beyond saving.

We concentrate today on the beginnings of the temple controversy proper, in 21:23–27, and the first two of the parables.

The group study passage (Matthew 21:23-27)

This first piece of concerted action by the chief priests and elders centres on the *authority of Jesus*. In fact, that is the theme of these chapters as a whole. This question of authority has two aspects.

• First, the question of divine sanction for acts of healing and for teaching. Who has God's authority and approval?

• But divine authority never exists in a vacuum. It is related to human, societal authority—in other words, the use of power. Who wields the power?

The Jewish authorities have religious power, and Jesus threatens that. They insist on putting the *power* issue first, whereas, for Jesus, the question of *the Father's authority and will* is primary (21:31). They refuse to acknowledge that Jesus is from God, simply because to recognize that would have unacceptable implications for the religious power they wield.

Jesus responds by questioning them about John the Baptist's authority. This isn't just a clever advocacy trick—though it is that!

• First, to respond by a question was a rabbinic teaching technique, designed, not to fox the enquirer, but to get him to probe issues for himself. The 'what do you think?' of verse 28 makes this clear. The leaders know the answer already—but are unwilling to acknowledge it.

• Secondly, to divert the question to the authority of John the Baptist is not a red herring. The question of John's and Jesus' authority is the same.

• Their message is the same—3:2; 4:17.

• John is Jesus' herald.

• Their destinies are similar: they are also aligned in terms of rejection and suffering: 17:10-13.

• Their estimation of the Jewish leaders is also identical: 3:7; 12:34.

If the leaders know the source of John's authority—which, in their hearts, they do—then they know the source of Jesus' authority!

The group study passage (Matthew 21:28-32)

This first parable is unique to Matthew. It achieves several aims:

• Coming after 21:23-27, where the answer to the leaders' question is left hanging in the air, this parable resolves that issue, and forces the chief priests and elders to answer.

• It answers the question 'Who is the true Israel?'

The parable works in much the same way as Nathan's parable in 2 Samuel 12. It sets up a scenario which doesn't at first appear to affect the hearers. But, too late, once the story has got under their guard, they realize that it addresses and challenges them! The same is also true about the second parable: 21:41.

The group study passage (Matthew 21:33–46)

The first parable has got under the hearers' skin, and they are ensnared, despite themselves, in the issues Jesus wants to address to them. So far, the leaders are told that tax collectors and prostitutes are going into the kingdom of heaven ahead of them: 21:31. This is *deliberately ambiguous*. It raises the question: do the Jewish leaders go second into the kingdom, or don't they get in at all? And the question is not answered!

This second parable more fully addresses the same issue—who is the true Israel? And it answers the question: the Jewish leaders will not get into the kingdom: 21:41; 21:43.

Unusually for Jesus, this parable is an allegory—a story where a number of the details are meant to represent characters or issues known to the hearers. See 'Verse-by-verse' for details.

The parable combines several themes: authority (21:34); abuse of authority (21:35); Jesus as Son of God (21:37); his passion (21:39); and the true Israel (21:41, 43). It has therefore a certain depth and richness.

Verse-by-verse

23 The questions 'by what authority?' and 'who gave you this authority?' show the double focus we discussed above. They can both be answered on different levels. On one level, the issue is 'did God give you this authority or not?'. On another level, the issue is 'you are trespassing on our preserve'.
'...these things...': does this refer to the entry into Jerusalem, the cleansing of the temple, Jesus' whole ministry, or to them all? The text is unclear.

29 A wordplay with verse 32, to set up a contrast. The same verb in Greek can mean 'to change one's mind' or 'to repent'. The first son changes his mind, and this results in obedience to his father. In verse 32, the Jewish leaders did not repent after seeing John the Baptist. In them, lack of response to John results in lack of repentance.

33 The vineyard is probably referring to Israel as the nation God chose for himself. Some commentators have argued that the vineyard represents the kingdom of heaven, but that is unlikely. The image of the vineyard stems from Isaiah 5:1f, and Isaiah 5:7 makes it clear that Israel is meant there. The landowner represents God; the tenants are contemporary Israel and its forebears.

34 'approached': the term here is used for 'the kingdom of heaven is at hand' in 3:2 and 4:17. The harvest, then, represents the coming-to-fruition of the kingdom of heaven.

35 Possibly a reference to the Former Prophets, namely (in the Hebrew Bible) the four books of Joshua, Judges, 1 and 2 Samuel (treated as one book), and 1 and 2 Kings (treated as one book).

36 Possibly refers to the Latter Prophets, namely the four books of Isaiah, Jeremiah, Ezekiel and the Twelve Minor Prophets (which count as one book).

37 The 'son' represents Jesus. 'My son' recalls Jesus' baptism and transfiguration, where he is called 'my beloved son'.

39 Unlike Mark 12:8, but like Luke 20:15, Matthew narrates that the son was killed outside the vineyard—a conscious reflection on the as-yet-future death of Jesus at Golgotha.

41 The 'other tenants' represent the church.

42 The quotation is from Psalm 118:22–23, in the Septuagint (Greek Old Testament) version. The connection between Jesus as the son (in the parable) and Jesus as the capstone (in the quotation) is uncertain. In Hebrew the terms for 'son' (*ben*) and 'stone' (*eben*) sound similar, and may have helped make the link.

6 Matthew 26:57–68; 27:1–2, 11–31

Religious and political trial

Aims

• To continue to look at Jesus' dealings with his opponents.

• To encounter Matthew's uncompromising views on the Jewish leaders and crowds and to struggle with their validity and meaning today.

• To meditate upon Jesus' mocking by the soldiers, his suffering and his crucifixion, and to allow these accounts to speak about authority, love and servanthood.

An important note

The question about 27:25 and the Jewish people needs thoughtful preparation and careful leading. All too often, passages such as this have been used as a platform for anti-Semitism, which is unacceptable wherever it is found. Whatever this verse signified to Matthew and his first readers, it cannot and must not be used today as a stick with which to beat the Jewish people. Leaders will need to be careful to avoid anything that might hint at apportioning blame for the crucifixion upon the Jewish people. Please be aware of this dimension as you lead this study. Please pay considerable attention to the verse-by-verse notes at 27:25.

That said, and said strenuously, it remains important to tackle this passage, difficult though it is: both because problem passages should not in principle be dodged, and because our relations with the Jewish people need to be reflected over since the Holocaust as never before.

The approach in this session is to lead people through the more cerebral parts of the study to the meditation on 27:27–31.

The group study passage (Matthew 26:57–68; 27:1–2, 11–31)

This is our third study in the third section of the Gospel of Matthew. This section runs from 16:21 to 28:20, and we have entitled it 'The passion and resurrection of Jesus'.

As we have seen, 16:21 acts as the introduction and heading to the whole section. The section expands upon 16:21. Today's passages, dealing with Jesus' trial before the Sanhedrin and Pilate and his mistreatment in both cases, certainly develops the first part of 16:21, where we are told that Jesus 'must suffer many things at the hands of the elders, chief priests and teachers of the law...'.

We have also noted that this introductory, summary passion prediction at 16:21 is repeated twice, in slightly different terms each time, in 17:22–23 and 20:17–19. That twofold repetition

acts as a sort of skeleton around which the third section of the Gospel is built. The repetition serves to keep the tension going. Like the first, these other passion predictions are also filled out by today's texts. 17:22 only briefly alludes to our passages. Of the three predictions, 20:17–19 is the most fully worked out in today's texts.

We have explored also how Matthew builds up the narrative to a climax through geographical focusing: as Jesus gets nearer to Jerusalem, so does his death and resurrection approach closer. The first and third passion predictions have foreshadowed the significance of Jerusalem in different ways. As we saw last time, Jesus has entered Jerusalem, and the conflict with the authorities has heightened. In today's passages, we reach the point where that conflict develops into formal trial proceedings in the heart of Jewish—and Roman—Jerusalem.

Apart from all this back-reference to passion predictions, there are also other resonances in our texts. The high priest's cross-examination brings to mind Peter's confession in 16:16. At the same time, it may refer back to Jesus' parable at 21:33f: see the verse-by-verse notes for this.

Finally, it is important to note the use of irony in these passages. We find it first in Caiaphas' questioning of Jesus: 26:63f. Until this point Jesus has remained silent. But then Caiaphas asks him a question about his identity. Surprisingly, he asks in similar terms to Peter's confession of faith in 16:16. So Caiaphas's question sounds like the sort of question a genuine enquirer would ask—whereas in fact he is, for Matthew, the arch-opponent of Jesus! He asks the *right* questions, for the *wrong* reasons and with the *wrong* motives, and is scandalized by Jesus' response. He and his associates, by convicting Jesus of 'blasphemy', show themselves up as 'blaspheming' opponents of the Messiah.

The second example is at Jesus' trial before Pilate. Pilate also asks Jesus the right question: 27:11. But again for the wrong reasons. There is irony here too. Pilate assists the Jewish conspiracy, but in doing so smoothes the way for the fulfilment of God's plan of salvation.

The third, and perhaps most telling, example of irony is the mocking by the soldiers. In their scathing attack upon Jesus, in which they dress him—and address him—as emperor, the soldiers are expressing, despite themselves, the truth about Jesus. *But he is not a king as they would have him. His sovereignty involves the willingness to give himself up to death.*

Verse-by-verse

26:59 '... were looking...': the imperfect tense suggests that they had been looking for some time.
'... false evidence...': Matthew adds the word 'false' to Mark 14:55, presumably to stress the intentions and responsibility of the Jewish authorities.

60 By virtue of Deuteronomy 17:6–7, the consistent evidence of two witnesses was required for a capital charge to be made out. The difficulty was probably in finding two consistent witnesses; see Mark 14:59, where we are told that not even these witnesses agreed.

63 Jesus' silence may be intended to bring Isaiah 53:7 and Psalm 38:12f to mind.
'I charge you...': this formula puts the witness on oath.
    Caiaphas's question comes as a surprise. First, nothing the witnesses have said testify to Jesus' claim to be Messiah or Son of God. Second, the question is put in *confessional* terms—in the sort of language an enquirer or a believer, not an accuser, would use of Jesus. For the reader, then, the question echoes Peter's similar confession of 16:16. See the overview above for further comment.

64 'You have said so': it is difficult to assess the tone of Jesus' reply here and at 27:11. According to Kingsbury and others, it is an *affirmative* statement. Jesus breaks his silence because Caiaphas has now come upon something which expresses the truth. According to Davies, Jesus is polite but evasive. Certainly Jesus' reply in Mark 14:62 seems more direct. Perhaps there is room for a middle way. Caiaphas—and Pilate—are right, but the implications of the fact that Jesus is Messiah, Son of God and King are not such as they would care to agree with. Hence Jesus agrees (since on one level their question has truth), but does so obliquely (because their reasons for asking are wrong). In effect, Jesus throws the question back at them. His response underscores the role of the questioner and hence heightens the irony. It 'makes the questioner an unintentional witness to the truth concerning which he asks' (Hare, page 315).

There is certainly strong irony here. Jesus' main enemy is the one who expresses the truth about him, however perversely. Jesus is to die for a truth which his accusers call 'blasphemy'. In

90

alleging 'blasphemy', the leaders profess that they know the thinking of God. However, they are wrong.

In any event, Jesus' reply continues more firmly. His words allude to Daniel 7 in particular. Matthew uses the Old Testament phrase 'Son of Man' to describe Jesus in terms of his relationship to the world, particularly as he interacts with the crowds and his opponents. These Old Testament references were understood to be messianic in tone. Jesus is referring to himself, by implication, as the Messiah.

66 'He is worthy of death': whether, strictly speaking, a charge of blasphemy—specifically cursing the Name of God, based on Leviticus 24:16—was made out on the evidence offered against Jesus is unclear. The exact charge may have been false prophecy. But, in a sense, this misses the point. Matthew is keen to inject irony into this encounter: the 'blasphemy' the authorities find in Jesus is in fact evidence of their own 'blasphemous' opposition to him.

27:11 The trial before Pilate is reported very briefly indeed. Pilate, like Caiaphas, makes Jesus' identity the issue.

Some ancient texts record that Barabbas was also called Jesus. This seems likely: such a detail would be more easily omitted (out of respect for Jesus' name?) than added. If so, Pilate's question in verse 17 becomes much more pointed.

20 The crowd have earlier hailed Jesus as the Son of David. Why have they changed their minds? Matthew puts responsibility for this upon the Jewish leadership.

22 Matthew here makes it crystal clear that Jesus is condemned as Messiah.

25 Matthew records Pilate's denial of responsibility and the crowd's acceptance of it so as to suggest that Jesus' death was primarily the responsibility of the Jews, though Pilate had been complicit in it. Matthew is making a polemical point here. He is interpreting the historical events. Clearly, historically speaking, the Romans were also responsible; otherwise Jesus would have been stoned, not crucified by Roman soldiers.

Matthew is highly critical of the Jewish people here. Yet, although Matthew blames the Jews for Jesus' death, it is vitally important not to let this passage—and particularly verse 25—become a source text for anti-Semitism. Matthew 5:43f will not allow this passage to be so misused. According to Matthew's theology, Israel as a nation has rejected the Messiah and in consequence is itself rejected as the vehicle and recipient of God's salvation. Verse 25 is an expression of that theological conviction. Harsh though this is, it *cannot justify the anti-Semitism* of which the Church has been guilty over the centuries. For a different view of the Jewish people as vehicle of God's continued purposes, read Romans 11.

27 In fact, the mocking of Jesus clearly demonstrates that responsibility for Jesus' crucifixion was Roman as well as Jewish.

Beyond this, the mocking of Jesus as king shows—again, ironically—exactly who Jesus is. See overview for further comment.

28 Scarlet was the colour of the soldiers' short cloaks. Mark and Luke have 'purple' here, the colour of the emperor's robes.

29 The crown of thorns was perhaps designed to cause pain; but more likely it was to represent the crown of the emperor.

7 The great commission

Aims

• To sum up our thoughts about Jesus' status, ministry and authority.

• To explore the theme of Jesus' universal authority.

• To explore the theme of universal mission and its ramifications today.

• To think about the presence of Jesus with the Church.

• To see how these three themes are interlinked, both in the passage and in our lives and ministries.

Important note

The study notes are deliberately shorter than usual—to leave room for things other than study in the last session. The passage is the whole of chapter 28; but the questions only directly cover verses 16–20. The leader's notes concentrate too on the last five verses. You might also wish to note that the 'Heart and Mind' course on Jonah (in the book on *Jonah and Exodus*) also considers the theme of mission.

The group study passage (Matthew 28:16–20)

This is our fourth and final study in the third section of Matthew's Gospel. We have noted—several times!—that each section of the Gospel…

• builds up to its own climax;

• builds on the work of the previous section, so that each section is a step up towards the final culmination of the whole Gospel.

So, together with the death of Jesus and the bystanders' acknowledgement of him as God's Son, the last five verses of Matthew are *doubly* a climax to his Gospel.

Within that climax, there is also a reference back to some of the opening verses of Matthew. The final words of Jesus in 28:20, where he promises to be with the disciples, mirror 1:23, where he is described as Emmanuel, 'God with us'. But they also enlarge upon the promise in 1:23—for we now have more of an idea how that promise of 'God with us' works out, and what it signifies.

One aspect of the passage is especially significant. In Matthew's Gospel, Jesus isn't reported as leaving his disciples. Things are left open-ended. As the Gospel closes, we are left with the image of Jesus addressing his disciples. 'I am with you always…' As we read these words, we, as well as the disciples, are being directly addressed by them. Bauer draws this conclusion: for Matthew, Jesus 'continues to dwell in the midst of his community [the church] in the time of the implied reader [that's us!]

just as truly as he 'dwells' with the disciples in the days of his earthly ministry... [He] continues to instruct and address his community now, just as he teaches his disciples on the Galilean hillside' (page 114).

And, according to Matthew, the Jesus who lives on in the Church isn't some sort of unearthly presence. He is the same Jesus who was with the disciples on earth. Matthew tells us this by forging links between this appearance of the risen Jesus and his earlier ministry. For instance, compare 28:18 and 11:25–27. The exalted Christ isn't some disembodied idea or projection in the disciples' minds, but the earthly Jesus himself.

Bauer (page 115) notes three themes which come to a climax in this passage: *Jesus' authority*, *universalism*, and *the presence of Jesus within the Church*.

Throughout our studies the question of *Jesus' authority* has been a major discussion point for Matthew. And here, in 28:18 is the obvious climax to that theme: 'all authority in heaven and on earth' has been given to Jesus, King, Son of God, God's Messiah, whom he has raised from death.

But authority over whom? There is a tension here in Matthew's Gospel. Earlier, Jesus instructed the disciples only to go to the 'lost sheep of the house of Israel' (15:24; see also 10:5–6). And, often, Matthew's references to Gentiles through the Gospel have been negative: 5:47; 6:7, 32; 18:17; 20:19, 25. Yet there are more positive hints and statements about the Gentiles, about Jesus' authority over them and the Church's mission to them. Chapter 1 includes Gentile women in Jesus' genealogy. The wise men come and worship. And the first clear indication that the Gentiles are included within the Church's ministry comes in 4:14–16. The faith of the centurion casts Gentiles in a positive light (8:10). Gentiles will share in the messianic banquet (8:11–12). Mission to the Gentiles is clearly in mind in 10:18. We find this strongly also in the parables against Israel (21:43 especially).

Indications of this *universalism* grow more intense in the passion narrative: 26:13, 28; 27:54. But, again, this theme reaches its peak in our passage. This isn't accidental. Just as we come across the most definitive statement of Jesus' universal authority, so we are given the strongest statement of the Church's universal mission. The two things are interlinked: see the 'therefore' of 28:19.

We have already noted that 'God with us' refers back to 1:23. But there is more than that here. The idea of 'God with us' has appeared also at 18:20, and at 26:29. But it comes to a high point in 28:20.

So Matthew tells us in this passage that Jesus has universal authority given to him, and that he exercises that authority in the midst of his people, the Church, in the context of the Church's mission. So this 'God with you' is not a comfortable feeling, or even just a feeling of security and safety. It is an assurance of *Jesus' presence* and authority as the Church goes out into the wider world.

But what kind of authority is it Jesus has? It is clear that Jesus' authority is the authority of the Son of God. We can see this because 28:16–20 is strongly linked with Son of God passages in Matthew's Gospel. 28:18 has strong verbal links with 11:27. Baptism in the name of Father, Son and Holy Spirit refers us back to Jesus' baptism at 3:16–17, where God calls him 'Son'.

To sum up, we can see these three themes—authority, universalism, the presence of Jesus—as forming a picture when taken together. Each is an aspect of the whole. Jesus' universal authority calls us to universal mission, and undergirds that mission. In that mission, we have Jesus' presence.

Kingsbury sums up the purpose of the passage as follows: 'to outline [the disciples'] ministry to the nations as the ambassadors of Jesus Son of God; to impress upon them that in this world they will live out their Christian existence between the poles of "doubt" and "worship"; and to assure them that they can always be certain of the saving presence of Jesus, in whom "God is with them"'.

Verse-by-verse

16 '...to the mountain...': a theological pointer, not just a geographical detail. Much happens on 'the mountain' in Matthew; teaching (5:1f); temptation (4:8); revelation (17:1f). 'The mountain' is, amongst other things, the place where Jesus' authority is revealed. So it is appropriate that Jesus' authority should be definitively revealed on 'the mountain'.

17 '...some doubted...': who does this apply to? Were only the eleven disciples present, or a wider core of believers? Tasker takes the former view, and interprets 'some doubted' as 'some at first doubted'; but this seems unlikely. If only the eleven disciples were there, it seems reasonable to understand this phrase as suggesting that there still remained within some of them residual doubts about Jesus. These words are a bit cryptic—but it is perhaps comforting to note that the apostles were human too!

18 We came across Daniel 7:13–14 in relation to 26:64, last time. There may be a further reference to it, and particularly Daniel 7:14, here.

20 This is the first time the disciples have been authorized to 'teach' by Jesus. This has been reserved to the end. They were not in a position until now to understand the nature and fulfilment of Jesus' ministry—his death and resurrection.

The emphasis on keeping Jesus' commands is typical of this Gospel: 6:14–15; 7:21–23. Davies comments: 'What is demanded of Jesus' followers is not passive acceptance of what he has achieved, but active participation in his way of life.'

94

READING RESOURCE LISTS

John's Gospel

C.K. Barrett, *The Gospel according to John*, SPCK, 1978

G.R. Beasley-Murray, *John*, Word, Waco, 1987

R.E. Brown, *The Gospel according to John*, IVP, 1991

D.A. Carson, *The Gospel according to John*, 2 volumes, Anchor Bible Commentaries, 1966 and 1970

S. Smalley, *John—Evangelist and Interpreter*, Paternoster, 1983

R.Schnackenburg, *John*, volume 1, Crossroad, New York, 1990

R.V.G. Tasker, *The Gospel according to St John*, Tyndale Commentaries, 1960

Matthew's Gospel

D.R. Bauer, *The Structure of Matthew's Gospel*, JSNT 31, Sheffield Academic Press, 1988

M. Davies, *Matthew*, 'Readings' Commentaries, JSNT Press, 1993

R.T. France, *Matthew*, Tyndale New Testament Commentaries

D.R.A. Hare, *Matthew*, Interpretation Commentaries, 1993

D. Hill, *The Gospel of Matthew*, New Century Bible Commentaries, 1972

J.D. Kingsbury, *Matthew: Structure, Christology, Kingdom*, Fortress Press, 1975

J.D. Kingsbury, *Matthew as Story*, Fortress Press, 1988

R.V.G. Tasker, *Matthew*, Tyndale New Testament Commentaries, 1961